Washington, DC Area by Area

Streetsmart

Within each Top 10 list in this book, no hierarchy of quality or popularity is implied. All 10 are, in the editor's opinion, of roughly equal merit.

Throughout this book, floors are referred to in accordance with American usage; i.e., the "first floor" is at ground level.

Front cover and spine *The iconic White House and its garden*
Back cover *Pedal boats on the Tidal Basin with Thomas Jefferson Memorial in the background*
Title page *The imposing marble statue of Abraham Lincoln in the Lincoln Memorial*

The information in this DK Eyewitness Top 10 Travel Guide is checked annually. Every effort has been made to ensure that this book is as up-to-date as possible at the time of going to press. Some details, however, such as telephone numbers, opening hours, prices, gallery hanging arrangements and travel information are liable to change. The publishers cannot accept responsibility for any consequences arising from the use of this book, nor for any material on third party websites, and cannot guarantee that any website address in this book will be a suitable source of travel information. We value the views and suggestions of our readers very highly. Please write to: Publisher, DK Eyewitness Travel Guides, Dorling Kindersley, 80 Strand, London WC2R 0RL, Great Britain, or email travelguides@dk.com

Welcome to
Washington, DC

City of politics and power. City of intrigue, passion, and history. World-renowned museums and monuments, broad avenues, vast green spaces, and breathtaking architecture combine to make this one of the most beautiful, captivating, and fun-to-explore cities in the world – and Eyewitness Top 10 Washington, DC puts it all at your fingertips.

What's not to love in a city where so much, including 18 Smithsonian museums and galleries, along with scores of monuments, memorials, and even government buildings, is open to the public free of charge? Everyone starts at the **National Mall**, the museum-and-monument-filled park that's the heart of the capital. You'll be able to discover dinosaurs and diamonds at the **National Museum of Natural History**; peruse Monets and Rembrandts in the **National Gallery of Art**; be moved by great words at the **Lincoln Memorial**; and see the city at your feet from the top of the **Washington Monument**.

Beyond the Mall, a cornucopia of theater, shopping, and adventure awaits you – from the legendary performances of the **Kennedy Center**, to the elegant boutiques of **Georgetown**, to the nightlife of **U Street** and **Adams Morgan**. And, of course, when you are ready to eat, you'll find the city overflowing with excellent restaurants serving international and local cuisines for every budget and palate.

Whether you're coming for a weekend or a week, our Top 10 guide is designed to bring together the best of everything the city can offer. It gives you tips throughout, from seeking out what's free to avoiding the crowds, plus six easy-to-follow itineraries, planned to tie together a clutch of sights in a short space of time. Add inspiring photography and detailed maps, and you've got the essential pocket-sized travel companion. **Enjoy the book, and enjoy Washington, DC**.

Clockwise from top: **Jefferson Memorial, Washington Monument, the North Apse in the Basilica of the National Shrine of the Immaculate Conception, the South Lawn of the White House, Martin Luther King, Jr. Memorial, quote from Franklin Delano Roosevelt Memorial, Georgetown Row Houses, Lincoln Memorial**

Exploring Washington, DC

Whether you have just a couple of days, or more time to explore, there's so much to see and do in America's capital city that you will want to make every minute count. The city is easy to get around on foot, with the Metrorail a fast and efficient alternative. Here are some ideas for how to make the most of your time.

Key
— Two-day itinerary
— Four-day itinerary

The White House is the residence of the President, as well as the seat of executive power.

Two Days in Washington, DC

Day ❶

MORNING
Start at the **National Air and Space Museum** (see pp20–21), then head to the **National Gallery of Art** (see pp24–7). Have lunch at **Pavilion Cafe** by the **National Sculpture Garden**.

AFTERNOON
Walk to the **White House** (see pp16–19) then stroll south to the **Washington Monument** (see p87), and west to the **Lincoln Memorial** (see p86) and the **Jefferson Memorial** (see p88). In the evening head to the **Kennedy Center** (see p99).

Day ❷

MORNING
Start early at the **National Museum of Natural History** (see pp28–9) then go next door to the **National Museum of American History** (see pp22–3).

AFTERNOON
Head to the Visitor Center of the **US Capitol** (see pp12–15) and take the

Capitol tour, followed by a stroll through the lush tropical landscapes within the **US Botanic Garden Conservatory** (see p80). Visit **Penn Quarter** (see p68) for dinner, then join the crowds ambling in the Mall to see the monuments lit up at night.

Four Days in Washington, DC

Day ❶

MORNING
Find out about the nation's story at the **National Museum of American History** (see pp22–3). Then stroll east on the Mall to the **National Gallery of Art** (see pp24–7) and have lunch in the **Cascade Cafe** (see p91).

AFTERNOON
Take the guided tour of the **Library of Congress** (see p79). Then head to the Visitor Center of the **US Capitol** (see pp12–15), and get a ticket for the tour.

The National Museum of Natural History captivates visitors, especially children, with its lively exhibits.

The White House
Nat. Museum of Natural History
National Sculpture Garden
Penn Quarter
Nat. Gallery of Art
US Capitol Visitors Center
Vietnam Veteran's Memorial
Lincoln Memorial
Washington Monument
Nat. Museum of American History
Nat. Air and Space Museum
Mitsitam Cafe
US Botanic Garden Conservatory
Library of Congress
Jefferson Memorial
Potomac

0 kilometers 1
0 miles 0.5

The Library of Congress is the largest in the world, housing over 120 million items in grand style.

Day ❷
MORNING
Visit the **National Air and Space Museum** (see pp20–21) early to avoid the crowds. Then cross the mall to the **National Museum of Natural History** (see pp28–9). Have lunch at **Mitsitam Cafe** in the **National Museum of the American Indian** (see p85).
AFTERNOON
Visit **The White House** (see pp16–19), then head south to the **Washington Monument** (see p87) past the **Vietnam Veterans Memorial** (see p86), to the **Lincoln Memorial** (see p86) and the **Jefferson Memorial** (see p88).

Day ❸
MORNING
Explore **Mount Vernon** (see pp36–9). Be sure to leave time to visit George Washington's grist mill and distillery.

AFTERNOON
Spend the afternoon at **Arlington National Cemetery** (see pp34–5). Head to **Old Town Alexandria** (see p111) for dinner.

Day ❹
MORNING
Early morning when the animals are active is the best time to explore the **National Zoological Park** (see pp32–3). Then visit the **National Cathedral** (see pp30–31) for a tour. Pause for lunch at **Two Amy's** (see p115).
AFTERNOON
Head to **Georgetown** (see pp104–7), stopping to explore the gorgeous gardens at **Dumbarton Oaks** (see p105). Then a short walk leads to great shopping all along Wisconsin and M streets. Finish with dinner at formal **1789** (see p109).

Top 10 Washington, DC Highlights

The US flag flies in front of the
United States Capitol

🔟 Washington, DC Highlights

The political, cultural, and spiritual heart of the United States, Washington, DC dazzles its visitors with stirring icons, noble monuments, and magnificent museums at every turn. A selection of the best the city has to offer is explored in the following chapter.

US Capitol ①

The Capitol's design combines ancient tradition and New World innovation, perfectly invoking the spirit of US democracy (see pp12–15).

② The White House

The most elegant and familiar of all the world's political residences, the White House has witnessed some of the most consequential decisions of modern history (see pp16–19).

③ National Air and Space Museum

Reportedly, this is the most visited museum in the world. The artifacts within trace one of mankind's greatest quests (see pp20–21).

National Museum of American History ④

A mix of "America's attic" and contemporary exhibits, ranging from political campaign buttons to historic examples of the Star-Spangled Banner (see pp22–3).

⑤ National Gallery of Art

The National Gallery's vast collection makes it one of the greatest art museums in the world (see pp24–7).

National Museum of Natural History

There's lots here to fascinate all ages, from the famous Rotunda elephant to the Hope Diamond and a Butterfly Pavilion *(see pp28–9)*.

Washington National Cathedral

Ancient and modern come together in this, the "national house of prayer," from the Gothic architecture to the Space Window *(see pp30–31)*.

National Zoological Park

Animals from across the world's varied habitats can be seen and studied at this internationally recognized leader in animal care, breeding of endangered species, and public education *(see pp32–3)*.

Mount Vernon

George Washington's estate and mansion is a perfect example of the gentleman-farmer roots of many of America's founding fathers *(see pp36–9)*.

Arlington National Cemetery

Four million people each year visit these rolling lawns studded with the headstones of America's war dead. A moving and reflective experience *(see pp34–5)*.

TOP 10 ★ United States Capitol

From its elevated site, described as "a pedestal waiting for a monument," the dignified Capitol has stood unwavering as the symbol of the American democractic process (an often rough-and-tumble one) throughout its more than 200-year history. The Capitol's frescoes and art collection qualify it as a notable museum, but its millions of tourists come, above all, to brush shoulders with history, both remembered and in the making.

Plan of the US Capitol

2 Capitol Dome
The central dome (below) defines the city for people worldwide. It was added, with the Statue of Freedom (see p15), between 1855 and 1866.

1 Capitol Visitor Center
The vast, underground Visitor Center (below) shows videos introducing Congress and the Capitol Complex, while the Exhibition Hall features displays and artifacts that recount the history of the Capitol.

3 Brumidi Corridors
Constantino Brumidi (1805–80) designed these ornate passageways on the lower floor of the Senate wing.

4 National Statuary Hall
The monumental *Liberty and the Eagle* by Enrico Causici (c.1819) overlooks this grand, semi-circular hall. The original House Chamber, it now displays statues of the nation's great and good.

7 Hall of Columns

This striking corridor **(right)**, more than 100 ft (30 m) long with lofty ceilings, is named after the 28 gracefully fluted white marble columns along its length. It houses additional items from the collection of the original House Chamber.

8 Columbus Doors

These imposing bronze doors, 17 ft (5 m) tall, are made up of reliefs picturing Christopher Columbus's life and his discovery of America. Designed by Randolph Rogers, the doors were cast in Munich in 1860.

5 Rotunda

America's first president ascends into the heavens in this 4,664-sq ft (430-sq m) fresco *The Apotheosis of Washington*, lining the interior of the dome **(above)**.

NEED TO KNOW

MAP R5 ■ National Mall, between 1st and 3rd Sts and Independence and Constitution Aves, SW ■ 202-226-8000 ■ www.visitthe capitol.gov

Open 8:30am–4:30pm Mon–Sat ■ Free (pass required for tours)

■ The new and impressive Visitor Center includes an Exhibition Hall, gift shop, restaurant, and gathering place for tours.

■ Security protocols forbid certain items to be carried on tours, including bulky bags and all foods, liquids, and aerosols; see www. visitthecapitol.gov for more details.

Capitol Guide
Current tours (bookable at www.visitthecapitol. gov) cover the historic sections in the center of the building, including the Rotunda, the National Statuary Hall, and the crypt. The galleries of the Senate and House of Representatives Chambers are open to the public when either body is in session. Cell phones, cameras, and other forms of recording device are not allowed in the galleries.

6 Senate Chamber

A semicircle of 100 desks faces the dais in this eminent assembly room. Democrats sit to the right, while Republicans are seated to the left.

9 House Chamber

The largest room in the Capitol is used for daily deliberations of the House of Representatives and for joint meetings of the House and Senate.

10 Old Senate Chamber

Used by the Senate from 1810 to 1859, this fine chamber **(left)** has been the setting for crucial debates on core issues in the development of the United States.

Events in the US Capitol's History

1 1787
The US Constitution authorizes the establishment of a federal district to be designated the official seat of the American government.

2 1791
George Washington selects the site for the new Capitol, with his city planner, Pierre Charles L'Enfant. They chose Jenkins Hill, 88 ft (27 m) above the north bank of the Potomac River.

3 1792
Dr. William Thornton wins a design contest for "Congress House," in which he proposed a simple central domed hall flanked by two rect-angular wings.

4 1800
Congress moves from Philadelphia to occupy the north wing of the Capitol.

5 1811
The Capitol is fully occupied by the House of Representatives and Senate, the Supreme Court, and Library of Congress.

British burn the Capitol in the War of 1812

George Washington

6 1814
British troops occupy the city and burn many buildings, including the Capitol, during the War of 1812 which lasted until 1815.

7 1818
Charles Bulfinch takes over restoration of the building and supervises its reconstruction. The Senate House and Supreme Court occupy new rooms by 1819, and the Rotunda is first used in 1824 to host a grand reception for General Lafayette.

8 1851
The Capitol is again damaged by fire. It is redesigned and rebuilt once more under the direction of Thomas U. Walter, who designs the cast-iron dome. Work continues on the Dome during the Civil War, while the Capitol is also used as a hospital, barracks, and bakery.

9 1880s–1900
Modern electrical lighting and the first elevator are installed. After another fire in 1898, fireproofing was at last installed.

10 1958–1962
The east front is extended 32 ft (10 m) east of the old sandstone front. The west front is restored between 1983 and 1987. This work produces the Capitol we see today.

Illustration of the US Capitol in 1852

THE STATUE OF FREEDOM

Crowning the Capitol dome stands Thomas Crawford's *Statue of Freedom*, commissioned in 1855. Freedom is depicted as a classical female figure, draped in flowing robes. Her Roman helmet, however, features the crest of an eagle's head, feathers, and talons, which some believe to be a reference to Native American dress. Crawford originally substituted the Roman helmet for the liberty cap, a symbol of freed slaves, but the then US Secretary of War, Jefferson Davis, objected. The statue faces east in accordance with the front of the building, not, to the puzzlement of many visitors, towards the rest of the nation. The east front was made the main building entrance simply because it faces an approach of level ground. This monumental symbol of liberty is 19.5 ft (6 m) tall and weighs around 15,000 lbs (6,800 kg). Sadly Crawford died in 1857, before it was erected.

The American Ideal
Although the *Statue of Freedom* may appear to face away from the heartland, she is nevertheless the embodiment of all Americans. Standing imperiously over the capital, and the nation as a whole, she encapsulates the notion of freedom for all citizens, laid out in the US Constitution. It is an ideal still fiercely protected today.

TOP 10
WORKS OF ART IN THE US CAPITOL

1 Statue of Freedom, Thomas Crawford (Dome)

2 The Apotheosis of Washington, Constantino Brumidi (Rotunda)

3 General George Washington Resigning His Commission, John Trumball (Rotunda)

4 Columbus Doors, Randolph Rogers (East Front)

5 Minton Tiles (floors and offices)

6 Brumidi Corridors (Senate Wing)

7 Statue to Lucretia Mott, Elizabeth Cady Stanton, and Susan B. Anthony, Adelaide Johnson (Rotunda)

8 Statuary (National Statuary Hall)

9 Declaration of Independence, John Trumball (Rotunda)

10 Baptism of Pocahontas, prior to her marriage to John Rolfe, Antonio Cappellano (Rotunda)

TOP 10 ⭐ The White House

Possibly the most famous residential landmark in the world, this dramatic Neo-Classical mansion has been the residence of the US president and family, the seat of executive power, and a working office building for over 200 years. Situated at the nation's most recognizable address, 1600 Pennsylvania Avenue, the White House reflects the power of the presidency. Its 132 rooms preserve and display the cultural settings of America's past and present. Lafayette Park to the north and the Ellipse to the south are good sites for viewing this American icon.

1 North Facade
The stately but welcoming main entrance on Pennsylvania Avenue **(below)** has a beautifully proportioned Ionic portico, added in 1829. Painted Virginia sandstone gives the building its white luster.

2 State Dining Room
As many as 140 guests may enjoy the president's hospitality in this formal dining room.

3 South Facade
The large semicircular portico added in 1824 dominates the south view **(right)**. The six main columns create an optical illusion, appearing to stretch from ground to roofline, emphasizing the classical proportions.

4 Map Room
Graceful Chippendale pieces furnish this private meeting room. Franklin D. Roosevelt adapted it as his situation room to assess the progress of World War II.

5 East Room
The East Room has been used chiefly for large receptions and ceremonial gatherings, such as dances, award presentations, press conferences, banquets, and historic bill and treaty signings.

6 Blue Room
The Blue Room **(below)** is by far the most elegant of all the reception rooms – it was George Washington who suggested its oval shape.

7 Oval Office
Since 1909 this illustrious room **(left)** has been the setting for the president's core tasks. Each leader adds his own touch – Barack Obama has added a bust of Martin Luther King, Jr. and examples of Native American pottery.

8 West Wing
This wing is the executive operational center of the White House, moved here in 1902 to allow more privacy in the main building.

9 Lincoln Bedroom
Although the name for this room **(below)** is a misnomer – Abraham Lincoln actually used it as an office – a number of his possessions are on display here.

NEED TO KNOW

MAP N4 ■ 1600 Pennsylvania Ave, NW (Visitor Center: 1450 Pennsylvania Ave, NW) ■ www.whitehouse.gov ■ Current information about tours can be obtained at 202-456-7041

Dis. access

■ If you have a telephoto lens or binoculars, the carved decorations on the north entrance and the Rose Garden, viewed from the Ellipse, deserve your attention.

■ The White House has no public restrooms. The nearest facilities are at the Visitor Center and the Ellipse Visitor Pavilion, near 15th and E streets.

Touring the White House
If you want to tour the White House, you must start the process well

before your visit. US citizens must request tickets from their Member of Congress. The request can be made up to 6 months in advance, but at the very minimum 21 days in advance. Tickets are limited and issued on a first come, first served basis. Foreign citizens must request the tickets from their embassy in DC.

These self-guided tours are available from 7:30a.m. to 11:30a.m. Tuesday through Thursday, 7:30a.m. to 1:30p.m. Fridays and Saturdays (excluding federal holidays).

For more information, including a list of prohibited items, visit www.whitehouse.gov/about/tours-and-events

You can also enjoy an interactive tour of the White House at www.whitehouse.gov/1600.

10 Visitor Center
The White House Visitor Center **(below)** has engrossing exhibits on various aspects of the mansion. It also offers park ranger talks, a souvenir shop, and special events such as military band concerts.

White House Decorative Features

Diplomatic Reception Room

1 Diplomatic Reception Room Wallpaper

The panoramic wallpaper is a series of large "Views of North America" printed in France in 1834.

2 China Room Collection

The White House collection of china services had grown so large by 1917 that Mrs Woodrow Wilson set aside a room in which to display it. Today, state and family china belonging to nearly every US president fills the handsome display cabinets.

3 Lighter Relieving a Steamboat Aground

This 1847 painting in the Green Room, by George Caleb Bingham, conveys the vitality of the nation.

4 Library

This former storage room was turned into a library in 1935, and contains a collection of books intended to reflect the philosophical and practical aspects of the presidency. Many pieces of the furniture in this room are attributed to the cabinet-maker Duncan Phyfe.

5 Monroe Plateau

James Monroe ordered a gilt table service from France in 1817. The plateau centerpiece is an impressive 14.5 ft (4.5 m) long when fully extended.

6 Grand Staircase

Descending to the Central Hall on the north side, the Grand Staircase is used for ceremonial entrances to state events in the East Room. Portraits of 20th-century presidents line the stairwell.

7 The Vermeil Room

"Vermeil" refers to the collection of gilded objects by early 19th-century silversmiths on display. Portraits of several First Ladies adorn the walls, and the room is grounded by one of the Empire-style tables purchased by President Andrew Jackson in 1829 for use in the East Room.

The Vermeil Room

8 Sand Dunes at Sunset, Atlantic City

This beach landscape (c.1885) by Henry Ossawa Tanner was the first work by an African American to be hung in the White House.

9 North Entrance Carvings

Scottish stonemasons created the fine carved surround for the north doorway with flowing garlands of roses and acorns.

Elegant table in the Library

10 Seymour Tall-Case Clock

This Oval Office clock ticks so loudly that its pendulum must be stopped when television broadcasts originate from the room.

PRESIDENT TRUMAN'S RENOVATIONS

Harry S. Truman

On moving into the White House, Harry S. Truman observed: "The floors pop and the drapes move back and forth," and "[t]he damned place is haunted, sure as shootin'." In 1948, after investigation, engineers confirmed that it was structural weakness, not ghosts, that was causing the problems. Some people said the house was standing "only from force of habit." The only solution was to move the First Family out and completely rebuild the White House within its external walls, gutting the inside entirely, and building a steel frame within the shell. Within it, the White House was recreated, room by room, from scratch. Most structural elements that can be seen today were built between 1948 and 1952, although a few earlier elements had been carefully dismantled and re-installed during reconstruction. America's three major networks broadcast the first-ever television tour of the residence in 1952. President Truman himself proudly led the tour and even entertained viewers by playing a tune on one of the pianos in the East Room *(see p16)*. A decade later, that arbiter of style Jacqueline Kennedy again restored many of the period features.

The White House was gutted in 1948 and completely rebuilt.

TOP 10 ★ National Air and Space Museum

This fascinating museum pays homage to some of the most ingenious and beautiful objects of flight, from the Wright brothers' biplane to powerful spacecraft. America by Air tells the story of America's airline industry from the formative years of mechanical flight. Compelling exhibitions put these historic objects in their social and political context. Actual moon rock is displayed so that the public can touch it.

1 Moving Beyond Earth

This exhibition explores the history and importance of human spaceflight in the US during the Space Shuttle and International Space Station era, interpreting the story of human spaceflight through artifacts, immersive experiences, and high-tech interactive kiosks.

2 1903 Wright Flyer

On December 17, 1903, Orville Wright flew this twin-winged craft **(left)** 120 ft (35 m), making it the first powered, piloted plane to be airborne. Muslin on a spruce and ash frame provided a light but strong body. The Wright brothers also designed the engine.

3 How Things Fly

Hands-on exhibits here lead visitors through the basics of flight, both human and animal, and explain forces that control flight of all types, from a helium balloon to a mission to Mars.

4 Looking at Earth

The focus here is on the contribution aerial photography **(above)** and space flight have given to our understanding of Earth. Many images are breathtakingly beautiful.

5 Skylab Orbital Workshop

This gold cylinder was an identical backup to the workshop that provided living and research space for the first US space station.

6 Apollo 11 Command Module Columbia

This vessel was the command center for the first lunar landing. It carried Neil Armstrong, Michael Collins, and "Buzz" Aldrin to the Moon and back.

7 WWI and WWII Aviation

A spectacular collection of Allied and Axis planes **(left)** from World Wars I and II, such as the Messerschmitt Bf 109 and the Supermarine Spitfire, makes this one of the most popular parts of the museum.

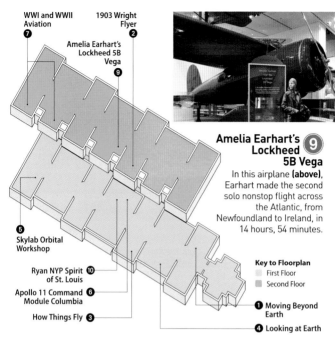

WWI and WWII Aviation ❼

1903 Wright Flyer ❷

Amelia Earhart's Lockheed 5B Vega ❾

Amelia Earhart's ❾ **Lockheed 5B Vega**
In this airplane **(above)**, Earhart made the second solo nonstop flight across the Atlantic, from Newfoundland to Ireland, in 14 hours, 54 minutes.

❺ **Skylab Orbital Workshop**

Ryan NYP Spirit of St. Louis ❿

Apollo 11 Command Module Columbia ❻

How Things Fly ❸

Key to Floorplan
◻ First Floor
◼ Second Floor

❶ Moving Beyond Earth
❹ Looking at Earth

❽ Steven F. Udvar-Hazy Center

This display area near Washington's Dulles Airport consists of two exhibition hangars. Opened to celebrate the 100th anniversary of the Wright brothers' first powered flight, it displays nearly 300 aircraft and spacecraft, including the space shuttle *Discovery*.

❿ Ryan NYP Spirit of St. Louis

Charles Lindbergh flew this plane on the first solo transatlantic flight, 3,610 miles (5,810 km) from Long Island to Paris in 1927. His 33-hour flight made him one of the most famous men of his age. The initials NYP in the plane's name stand for New York–Paris.

NEED TO KNOW

MAP Q5 ▪ Independence Ave, 6th St, SW ▪ 202-633-1000 ▪ www.nasm.si.edu

Open 10am–5:30pm daily; closed Dec 25

Dis. access

Museum: Free

Planetarium and theater shows: adults (13–59 years) $9.00, seniors (over 60 years) $8.00, youths (2–12 years) $7.50, Smithsonian members $6.50

Steven F. Udvar-Hazy Center: 14390 Air and Space Museum Pkwy, Chantilly, VA 20151

▪ McDonald's, Boston Market, and Donato's Pizzeria are located in the greenhouse-like extension on the east end of the building.

▪ The museum features in the 2009 film *Night at the Museum 2: Battle of the Smithsonian*, starring Ben Stiller.

Museum Guide

Entrances to the museum are on Independence Ave and the Mall. Both lead into the spacious central hall where the most famous airplanes of all time are displayed. An information booth is near the Independence Ave entrance. To see a film at the Lockheed Martin IMAX Theater or the Albert Einstein Planetarium, obtain tickets on arrival at the museum, or buy them in advance online.

TOP 10 ⭐ National Museum of American History

Three huge floors filled with a variety of fascinating objects make up this paean to American culture. The first floor focuses on science and technology, including hands-on experiments and exhibitions on transport, electricity, and machinery. The second floor is home to the famous Star-Spangled Banner, while the third floor features a stirring tribute to the American presidency and military history.

1 The Price of Freedom: Americans at War
This gallery explores the nation's military history, from the French and Indian War in the 1750s to recent conflicts in Afghanistan and Iraq.

2 American Stories
A collection of wonderful artifacts from the world of popular entertainment, including Dorothy's ruby slippers from *The Wizard of Oz*, Kermit the Frog, and other favorites from the worlds of entertainment and sports.

3 John Bull Locomotive
The oldest still-operable, self-propelled vehicle in the world, the John Bull locomotive was built in England and brought to America in 1831. The only one of its kind, it transported passengers between Philadelphia and New York on the Camden and Amboy Railroad between 1831 and 1866.

4 The First Ladies at the Smithsonian
The First Ladies' gallery is a firm favorite and includes inaugural gowns worn by Jackie Kennedy, Nancy Reagan, Frances Cleveland **(left)**, Michelle Obama, and many others.

5 FOOD: Transforming the American Table 1950–2000
A meticulous recreation of Julia Child's kitchen **(above)** opens this exploration of the significant changes in the production and consumption of food and wine in postwar America.

6 Gunboat Philadelphia
In October 1776, the *Philadelphia* was sunk by the British during a battle on Lake Champlain on the US–Canadian border, and rested on the bottom of the lake until it was recovered in 1935. It came to the museum in 1964, complete with its equipment and the 24-pound ball that sent the gunboat to the bottom.

10 Within These Walls...

A two-storey colonial house from Massachusetts has been rebuilt within the museum, to explore the 200-year history of the families who lived there.

7 The Star-Spangled Banner

The flag that inspired the national anthem (above) is strikingly large – originally 30 by 42 ft (9 by 13 m) – although timeworn. Created by Baltimore flag-maker Mary Pickersgill in 1813, it is in a gallery that recreates the Battle of Baltimore and the burning of the White House.

Key to Floorplan

First floor
Second floor
Third floor

4 The First Ladies

6 Gunboat Philadelphia

The Price of Freedom 1

8 America on the Move

Multimedia presentations and other theatrical techniques tell the story of America's transportation since 1876. The vast exhibition holds over 340 objects, such as an 1897 gasoline tricycle.

Within These Walls 10

The Star-Spangled Banner 7

2 American Stories

The American Presidency 9

John Bull Locomotive 3

America on the Move 8

FOOD 5

9 The American Presidency

Highlights include the portable desk at which Jefferson wrote the Declaration of Independence, and the top hat (above) Lincoln was wearing the night he was assassinated.

NEED TO KNOW

MAP P4 ■ 14th St and Constitution Ave, NW
■ 202-633-1000 ■ www.americanhistory.si.edu

Open 10am–5:30pm daily; extended hours in summer; closed Dec 25

Dis. access

■ The Stars and Stripes Café and Constitution

Café are located within the museum and offer a variety of dishes.

Museum Events
An amazing variety of events, both entertaining and enlightening, are available to the public. Phone ahead or check online for updates. Try out some of the interactive exhibits, or take part in debates on controversial issues. One highlight is a section of the original Woolworth's lunch counter from Greensboro, NC, a landmark from the Civil Rights Movement, when African-Americans sat at this "whites only" counter asking to be served. At regular intervals you are invited to relive the events of 1960.

🔟⭐ National Gallery of Art

The collections at this immense gallery rival those of any art museum in the world, displaying milestones of Western art from the Middle Ages to the 20th century and including Italian Renaissance works, Dutch Masters, French Impressionists, and all ages of American art. John Russell Pope designed the harmonious Neo-Classical West Building in 1941.

④ The Adoration of the Magi

This festive view of the Magi at Christ's birthplace **(left)** was painted in tempura on a circular panel by Fra Angelico and Filippo Lippi in about 1445.

⑤ Watson and the Shark

The dramatic subject matter, muscular painting, and expressions of dread and anxiety meant that this John Singleton Copley painting caused a sensation when it was first displayed in 1778.

① Calder Mobile, East Building

Alexander Calder's swooping structure, his last major work (installed in 1977), dominates the atrium of the I.M. Pei-designed East Building.

③ Ginevra de' Benci

The careful modeling of lustrous flesh against juniper foliage make this Leonardo da Vinci canvas of 1474, his only one in the US, a lively but composed work.

② Wivenhoe Park, Essex

Light and shade, the perception of calm, and clarity of detail create an absorbing landscape **(below)**. In this 1816 work, John Constable demonstrates his love of the English countryside.

⑥ Girl with the Red Hat

This 1665 portrait **(above)** shows off Johannes Vermeer's striking use of color: yellow highlights in the blue robe, purple under the hat, turquoise in the eyes. The luminosity is enhanced by the smooth panel base.

9 The River of Light
Frederick Edwin Church's 1877 oil painting of the Amazon is based on sketches taken during a trip to South America. This otherworldly work emphasizes the power of nature.

7 Right and Left
The title of Winslow Homer's 1909 painting **(above)** refers to shooting ducks with separate barrels of a shotgun. The fleeting nature of the ducks' existence echoes our own.

Ginevra de' Benci **3** **4** The Adoration of the Magi

The Alba Madonna **8**

Girl with the Red Hat **6**

10 Portraits of the First Five Presidents
This is the only complete set of Gilbert Stuart's five paintings (1817–21), including George Washington **(above)**, still in existence. Another set was partially destroyed by fire in 1851 at the Library of Congress.

Wivenhoe Park, Essex **2**

8 The Alba Madonna
Unusually, the Madonna in Raphael's 1510 work is shown seated on the ground. The composition is serene, but it shows Christ accepting the cross from St. John the Baptist, a precursor of events to come.

5 Watson and the Shark

10 Portraits of the First Five Presidents

7 Right and Left

9 El Rio de Luz (The River of Light)

1 Calder Mobile, East Building

NEED TO KNOW

MAP Q4 ▪ 3rd–7th Sts at Constitution Avenue NW
▪ 202-737-4215
▪ www.nga.gov

Open 10am–5pm Mon–Sat, 11am–6pm Sun; closed Dec 25, Jan 1

Dis. access

▪ The Cascade Café, located between the West and East Buildings, has an espresso bar, while the Pavilion Café in the Sculpture Garden is an great spot to grab a bite.

▪ From 2014–16 the East Wing is being expanded, adding a new, skylit fourth level and out-door sculpture terrace.

Gallery Guide
The first floor contains European paintings and sculpture, and American art. The ground floor displays works on paper, sculpture, decorative arts, and temporary exhibits. The location of works changes periodically. An underground concourse leads to the East Building.

National Gallery of Art Collections

The Dance Lesson, by Edgar Degas

1 French 19th-Century Paintings

Especially rich in Impressionist works, this collection includes some of the world's most beloved works of art, such as Monet's *Japanese Footbridge* and Degas' *Four Dancers* and *The Dance Lesson* (1879).

2 American Paintings

The breadth of this collection reveals many interesting themes: portraiture, a desire for accuracy in depicting American life and landscape, and a social conscience.

3 Italian 13th- to 15th-Century Paintings

Best known for the increasing mastery of the naturalistic portrayal of the human figure and of interior and exterior settings, the works in this extensive collection still have appealing variety: decorative, mystical, simple, and elegant.

4 Italian 16th-Century Painting

The mature flowering of the Renaissance bursts forth in this broad collection of works by Raphael, Giorgione, Titian, and many others.

5 Works on Paper

The National Gallery is especially strong in this area. Repeat visitors see an almost unbelievable quantity and variety of exquisite drawings, prints, illustrated books, and photographs. The permanent collection contains more than 65,000 items, dating as far back as the 11th century.

6 Dutch and Flemish Paintings

Again, visitors will find an overwhelmingly rich array of Old Master works by artists such as Rembrandt, Frans Hals, Van Dyck, Rubens, Vermeer, and their contemporaries.

7 Spanish Paintings

El Greco, Zurbarán, Murillo, and Velázquez are just some of the 18th- to 19th-century highlights in this vibrant collection.

8 Decorative Arts

Sumptuous tapestries, full of imagery, outstanding pieces of furniture, and everyday items such as Chinese porcelain plates and bowls, give a wonderful glimpse of the passing centuries in Europe.

Collections Floorplan
■ First floor
■ Second floor

9 European Sculpture

Portrait busts and portrait medals have always been important products of the sculptor's studio, and many fine examples are displayed here. There is also an especially absorbing selection of Rodin's work and some interesting experimental sculptural pieces by Degas.

10 Painting and Sculpture of the 20th Century

The frantic rate of change in 20th-century art is laid out here – from Matisse's Fauvist works, the Cubists Picasso and Braque, the abstraction of Mondrian, and Surrealists such as Magritte and Miró, right up to Minimalism and Pop Art.

THE EAST BUILDING AND SCULPTURE GARDEN

The East Building is an angular construction designed to house permanent and touring exhibitions of contemporary art. Its entrance is from 4th Street or from the underground concourse leading from the West Building. A huge orange-and-black mobile by Alexander Calder dominates the lobby, while exhibition rooms line the outer walls of the upper halls, connected by hanging crosswalks. The exhibition space is being renovated and reopens to the public in late 2016; the lobby area remains open. The Sculpture Garden is a lively public space integrating contemporary art with beautifully landscaped gardens and a relaxing reflection pool with its spraying central fountain. In the 6-acre (2.5-ha) block next to the West Building, the garden includes plantings of native species of trees, shrubs, and perennials, along with 17 pieces from the Gallery's collection and several items on loan from other museums. There are free jazz concerts in the summer on Fridays, and the pool transforms into a popular ice-skating rink in winter.

TOP 10 WORKS IN THE SCULPTURE GARDEN

1 **Puellae (Girls)**, Magdalena Abakanowicz (1992)

2 **House I**, Roy Lichtenstein (1996–8)

3 **Four-Sided Pyramid**, Sol LeWitt (1997)

4 **Graft**, Roxy Paine (2008)

5 **Personnage Gothique**, Oiseau-Éclair, Joan Miró (1974)

6 **Six-Part Seating**, Scott Burton (1985–98)

7 **Spider**, Louise Bourgeois (1996)

8 **Thinker on a Rock**, Barry Flanagan (1997)

9 **Chair Transformation Number 20B**, Lucas Samaras (1996)

10 **Moondog**, Tony Smith (1964–99)

Seating in the Sculpture Garden

TOP 10 ⭐ National Museum of Natural History

From Marie Antoinette's earrings to the giant jaws of a pre-historic shark, this museum is full of fascinating treasures collected by Smithsonian scientists for over a century. Ancient mummies, rare gems and minerals, previously unknown plants and animals, and the bones of mighty dinosaurs are on display, making this one of the most popular museums on the Mall.

3 African Elephant
This huge bull elephant **(left)** seems to fill the Rotunda and has become a symbol of the museum itself. Weighing in at over 8 tons, this was the largest land animal on display when it was unveiled in 1959. Exhibits on the second-floor balcony tell the story of African elephants.

4 Fossil Lab
Look through the windows into a genuine fossil lab where museum scientists clean, prepare, and mount fossils from around the world that have recently been collected by scientists.

5 Orkin Insect Zoo
All kinds of insects can be viewed in their natural habitats. Volunteers do tarantula feedings and offer children a chance to touch and hold live insects each day.

1 Hope Diamond
Not the world's largest diamond, but certainly the most famous, and possibly the most viewed artifact in any museum in the world. The 45.52 carat deep-blue diamond **(left)** was part of the French Crown Jewels, and is reputed to be cursed.

2 The Last American Dinosaur
The museum's legendary Dinosaur Hall is under-going major reconstruc-tion lasting until 2019. In the meantime, dinosaur fans can view this special exhibit that highlights the large dinosaurs that roamed the earth just before a global catas-trophe ended their reign.

6 Hall of Mammals
From a roaring African lion **(above)** to an enormous Grizzly Bear standing on its hind legs, this hall is filled with dramatic representations of warm-blooded animals from around the world.

7 Butterfly Pavilion

A family favorite, this pavilion offers the chance to stroll among fluttering beauties with fanciful names like Gulf Fritillary **(left)** and Madagascar Moon Moth.

8 Ptolomaic Mummy

This mummy of a 40-year-old man who died over 2,000 years ago is the star of "Eternal Life in Ancient Egypt." Displays include a step-by-step guide to the process of mummification.

- **4** Fossil Lab
- **2** The Last American Dinosaur
- **8** Ptolomaic Mummy
- **1** Hope Diamond
- **5** Orkin Insect Zoo
- **7** Butterfly Pavilion
- **9** Right Whale
- **3** African Elephant
- **6** Hall of Mammals
- **10** Neanderthal Man

Key to Floorplan
- Ground floor
- First floor
- Second floor

ORIGINS OF THE SMITHSONIAN

The world's largest museum complex, the Smithsonian Institute was founded in 1826 when British scientist James Smithson left half a million dollars (about $15 million today) "to found in Washington, under the name of the Smithsonian Institution, an establishment for the increase and diffusion of knowledge among men." Today, the Smithsonian Institute in Washington comprises 19 museums, 9 research centers, and a zoo, and every one of its public venues can be entered free of charge.

9 Right Whale

The life-size model hanging from the ceiling of the impressive Hall of Oceans is of a real whale named Phoenix that the Smithsonian has tracked since 1987.

10 Neanderthal Man

The result of painstaking forensic and reconstruction work, this life-size head is one of many artifacts exploring the evolution of humans.

NEED TO KNOW

MAP P4 ■ 10th St and Constitution Ave., NW
■ 202-633-1000
■ www.mnh.si.edu

Open 10am–5:30pm daily; closed Dec 25; National Fossil Hall: Closed for renovation until 2019

Dis. access

Free (Butterfly Pavilion: adm by timed ticket, book online; free Tue)

■ The Atrium Café offers locally sourced vegetables and hormone-free meats, in the form of burgers, pizzas, deli sandwiches, and other family-pleasing meals. Dining early is recommended as this is a busy eatery after midday.

■ Teens and tweens will enjoy Q?rius (pronounced curious), an interactive learning space that connects science with everyday life. The center is open to the public from July through September from 10am to 5pm.

■ If you want a quieter museum experience, it's a good idea to plan on visiting from Monday to Wednesday. Saturday is the busiest day of the week.

🔟⭐ Washington National Cathedral

This Gothic building is the focus of public spiritual life. The sixth largest cathedral in the world, it was completed in 1990, with a 10-storey-high nave and a central tower 676 ft (206 m) tall, the highest point in the District of Columbia. This Episcopal church is officially named the Cathedral Church of Saint Peter and Saint Paul.

⑥ Main Entrance and Creation

The west entrance is centered within a high Gothic arch containing a lovely rose window. Sited above the huge bronze double doors is *Ex Nihilo,* a relief sculpture by Frederick Hart, which portrays the creation of humankind from chaos.

South Rose Window ①

"The Church Triumphant" is the theme of this elegant stained-glass rose window **(right)**. The design of Joseph G. Reynolds incorporates 12 brilliantly colored "petals" and numerous other figures. It is mirrored by the North Rose window.

② Space Window

This stained-glass window by Rodney Winfield is notable for commemorating mankind's 20th-century moon landing. A piece of moon rock, brought back by Apollo 11 astronauts, is embedded in it.

Exterior ③

The architecture of the cathedral is predominantly English Gothic, created using authentic methods dating from the Middle Ages, including a cross-shaped floorplan, flying buttresses, and spired towers **(right)**.

④ Pipe Organ

This magnificent Aeolian-Skinner instrument has 10,650 pipes. On most Mondays and Wednesdays at 12:30pm, an organist gives a presentation and then demonstrates with a mini-recital.

⑤ Nave

The vertical impression given by the nave **(left)** is also typical of English Gothic style. Flags of the states are often displayed around the outer walls.

Cathedral floorplan

7 Gardens

A medieval walled garden is the model for the cathedral's beautiful Bishop's Garden **(right)** on the south side of the church. The herb gardens are a delight to the nose as well as the eye: all the stones here originated in a quarry that George Washington once owned.

BUILDING THE CATHEDRAL

In 1893, Congress granted a charter to construct Washington National Cathedral. Theodore Roosevelt attended the laying of the foundation stone at the Mount St. Albans location in 1907. The stone was brought from a field near Bethlehem. The completion of the west towers in 1990 marked the end of 83 years of continuous work. In 2011, the cathedral was severely damaged by an earthquake and works to stabilize the structure continue.

8 High Altar

The imposing high altar at the east end of the magnificent nave is made from stone dug from Solomon's quarry outside Jerusalem.

NEED TO KNOW

MAP H4 ■ Massachusetts & Wisconsin Aves NW
■ 202-537-6200 ■ www.nationalcathedral.org

Open 10am–5:30pm Mon–Fri, 10am–4pm Sat, 7:45am–4pm Sun (weekend hours subject to change)

Dis. access

Adm $11 adults; $7 senior citizens & youth 5–17yrs; free under 5 yrs & for services and worship.

- The cathedral offers live music concerts year-round.
- Binoculars or a telephoto lens are a must for appreciating the gargoyles and grotesques.

9 Gargoyles and Grotesques

Derived from decorated spouts on European buildings, these carved ornaments have been given free rein at the cathedral. The 112 carvings include Darth Vader and a predatory-looking snake.

10 Children's Chapel

This endearing room is child-scaled, with a miniature organ and altar and chairs to fit six-year-olds. Jesus is also shown as a boy in the sculpture here.

TOP 10 ★ National Zoological Park

Opened in 1889, and one of the most visited destinations in Washington, the Smithsonian's National Zoo is a beautifully landscaped 163-acre (66-ha) urban park and an innovative center for animal care and conservation. Children and adults delight at seeing rare giant pandas, endangered Asian elephants, and majestic tigers. More than 2,000 animals live here, increasingly housed in habitats that allow natural behavior.

1 Great Cats

The endangered Sumatran tiger has been successfully bred at the National Zoo. Nearby are lions, caracals, and cheetahs **(right)**; visit the Asia Trail to see leopards and Southeast Asian fishing cats.

3 Giant Pandas

Mei Xiang and Tian Tian, two giant pandas **(left)** on loan from China, made their first appearance at the zoo in 2001 as part of a research and conservation program. Their cub, Bao Bao, is the newest addition. Their social interactions and physical beauty are fascinating.

4 Cheetah Conservation Station

Cheetahs and zebras (separated by a fence) display natural behaviors in a grassland setting shared with gazelles and other African savanna-dwellers.

5 Bird House and Outdoor Flight Cage

Here, numerous species of birds display spectacular colors and elegant motions. The cage is a netted structure that gives even birds of prey enough room to show off.

2 Reptile Discovery Center

The center's 70 reptile and amphibian species include snakes, turtles, frogs, and the Komodo dragon, a venomous Indonesian lizard that can grow as large as 200 lbs (90 kg) and 10 ft (3 m) long.

NEED TO KNOW

MAP J4 ■ 3001 Connecticut Ave, NW ■ 202-633-4888 ■ www.nationalzoo.si.edu

Open Apr–Oct: grounds 6am–8pm, buildings 10am–6pm daily; Nov–Apr: grounds 6am–6pm, buildings 10am–4:30pm daily; closed Dec 25 ■ From Jun–Sep, the Snore and Roar sleepover allows visitors to take a nocturnal tour and camp in the zoo grounds

Dis. access

■ Most children's tour groups arrive between 10am and noon in the fall. Visit the giant pandas after 2pm.

National Zoological Park Plan

⑦ Great Apes

Western lowland gorillas **(left)** are among our closest relatives, sharing about 98 percent of our genes. Their movements and human-like manner mesmerize observers. The primates are outdoors in the mornings and mid-afternoons.

⑧ Asian Elephants

One of the most popular exhibits at the zoo is Elephant Trails. This state-of-the-art enclosure recreates the elephants' natural home, featuring unique outdoor and indoor habitats.

⑥ Asia Trail

It's home to sloth bears, clouded leopards, fishing cats, otters, red pandas, a Japanese giant salamander, and giant pandas.

ZOO HORTICULTURE

The zoo's lush parklands are far more than just pleasant surroundings for its visitors. In the Amazonia exhibit, for example, living avocado and cocoa trees help to re-create the tropical environment of this diverse river basin, while a cheetah wanders around a re-creation of the grasslands of its native African habitat.

⑨ Kid's Farm

Home to alpacas, cows, donkeys, and goats, as well as some rare breeds, this exhibit gives children the opportunity to pet and groom the animals. There is also a giant playground for kids to let off steam.

⑩ Amazonia

This exhibit **(above)** recreates the tropical habitat of the Amazon basin and features a variety of animals, including poison arrow frogs, titi monkeys, and a two-toed sloth.

TOP 10 ⭐ Arlington National Cemetery

Some of America's most cherished burial sites are found in the nation's best-known military cemetery. The rolling lawns filled with white tombstones, the Tomb of the Unknowns, and the grave of John F. Kennedy are conspicuous symbols of sacrifices made for freedom. The flags fly at half-staff from before the first and after the last of 25–30 funerals per day, as the graves of veterans continue to multiply. Nearly four million people visit the cemetery every year.

① Lawns of Graves

Approximately 350,000 people are buried on these grounds, marked by simple graves, arranged in regular grids, spread across the lawns **(right)**. Although only a small percentage of America's war dead lie here, the expanse gives a tangible picture of the human cost of war.

④ Memorial Amphitheater

This marble amphitheater **(left)** is the setting for the Memorial Day and Veterans' Day ceremonies (see p73), when the nation's leaders pay tribute to those who have served their country.

② Confederate Memorial

Although the cemetery is often thought to be only for Union soldiers, 482 Confederate soldiers are buried here too, around a central memorial.

③ Tomb of Pierre L'Enfant

Honoring the designer of the Washington city grid (see p42), L'Enfant's monument shows his magnificent plan of the city within a circle.

⑤ Arlington House

This impressive mansion was conceived as a memorial to George Washington, built by his adopted grandson.

⑥ Tomb of the Unknowns

This solemn monument **(right)** is guarded 24 hours a day by the Old Guard. Unknown soldiers of World Wars I and II and the Korean War are here. A Vietnam soldier was interred here, but he was later identified.

7 Rough Riders Memorial

This granite memorial **(left)** displays the insignia of the First US Volunteer Cavalry (the "Rough Riders") and the battles they fought during the Spanish–American War.

CIVIL WAR ORIGINS

Robert E. Lee lived in Arlington House until 1861, when tensions between the Union and the Southern states reached a crisis. When Virginia joined the Confederacy and seceded from the Union, Lee became a general of Virginia's military forces. Union troops then crossed the Potomac and took possession of Arlington House. In 1864, Arlington National Cemetery was created to cope with the mass deaths of the Civil War.

8 Seabees Memorial

A bronze construction worker pauses to make friends with a young child. The Seabees (the Construction Battalion) performed daring feats in building the military bases needed to win World War II.

9 Shuttle Memorials

One memorial honors the astronauts who died in the space shuttle *Challenger* disaster in 1986. Another, to the crew lost in the 2003 *Columbia* shuttle tragedy, is nearby.

10 Grave of John F. Kennedy

The eternal flame on the grave **(above)** of the assassinated president was lit by Jacqueline Kennedy on the day of his funeral. In 1994, she was buried beside him.

NEED TO KNOW

MAP K6 ▪ Arlington, VA ▪ 703-607-8000
▪ www.arlington cemetery.org

Open Apr–Sep: 8am–7pm daily; Oct–Mar: 8am–5pm daily

Dis. access

Free; ANC tourbus tickets: adults $8.75, children (3–11) $4.75, seniors (65 years and over) $7.75; Free shuttle to graves.

▪ The ANC tour bus departs from the Welcome Center throughout the day. The tour is accompanied by a commentary and includes stops at major sites.

Plan of Cemetery

🔟 ⭐ Mount Vernon

This graceful mansion, on the banks of the Potomac River, is the second most visited historic residence in America after the White House. George Washington inherited the estate aged 22, and lived at Mount Vernon for over 40 years. With many of the buildings and activities brought back to life, no other place better portrays the character of the first US president, or the role of slavery-based agriculture in the young republic.

6 Large Dining Room

This impressive two-storey room **(below)** is formal enough for state business yet is inviting to all. Washington used boards placed on trestles for a table – easier to clear for dancing.

1 Mansion's Exterior

The huge portico **(above)** that overlooks the Potomac was the president's own design. The house is pine, but the exterior was "rusticated" with a treatment that re-creates the look of stone.

2 Nelly Custis Room

Martha Washington's granddaughter, Nelly Custis, lived at Mount Vernon from early childhood. This comfortable room was hers; she even stayed here for a short while after she had married.

3 Little Parlor

Many visitors find this pretty room **(right)** a highlight of the mansion because it reflects the family life lived in the house. The original harpsichord Washington purchased for his step-granddaughter, Nelly Custis, is displayed.

4 Front Parlor

This charming parlor was one of George Washington's favorite rooms in the house, and he had it decorated in stylish Prussian blue paint, with an English Wilton carpet. A portrait of him, by Charles Willson Peale, hangs here.

5 Master Bedroom

Often called Mrs. Washington's Room, this is where George and Martha slept. Mrs. Washington ordered the oversized mahogany bed in the 1790s.

9 Kitchen

Mrs. Washington directed a staff of slaves in the kitchen **(left)**, and at least two cooks' names have survived, Nathan and Lucy. Much physical labor was required for cooking – fuel and water had to be hauled in by hand.

7 Lafayette Bedroom

This guest bedroom, with its beautiful view of the Potomac, is one of five and is where the Marquis de Lafayette, one of Washington's military aides and a lifelong friend, would stay.

10 Study

This room was the setting for Washington's commercial, political, and public work. It was also his dressing room, where he would wash and shave, and a place of retreat from the bustle of the household.

BUILDING MOUNT VERNON

The estate that was to be Mount Vernon had been in the Washington family since 1674. George Washington inherited the estate in 1754 and in the succeeding years built up the property and grounds. Additions to the house were underway at the beginning of the Revolutionary War, but the dining room was completed after the war.

NEED TO KNOW

3200 Mount Vernon Parkway ▪ 703-780-2000 ▪ www.mountvernon.org

Open Apr–Aug: 8am–5pm daily; Mar, Sep, Oct: 9am–5pm daily; Nov–Feb: 9am–4pm daily

Dis. access

Adm $17 adults; $16 senior citizens; $9 children 6–11 years; free under 6 yrs.

▪ Re-enactments are held throughout the year. See website for details and dates.

▪ The Mount Vernon shops sell seeds of some of the estate's heritage plants.

▪ Outside the main entrance is a complex with a full-service restaurant, the Mount Vernon Inn, offering specialties such as peanut and chestnut soup and salmon corncakes, as well as a food court, serving snacks.

Key to Floorplan

- First floor
- Second floor
- Third floor

8 Cupola

The cupola, with its "dove-of-peace" weathervane, provides light to the third floor and aids air circulation in summer.

Mount Vernon Grounds

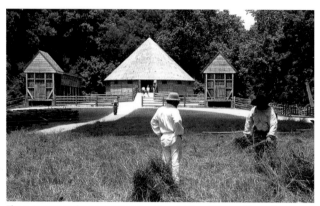

The reconstructed 16-Sided Treading Barn in Mount Vernon Grounds

1 16-Sided Treading Barn

With this unique design, George Washington created one of the most aesthetically pleasing and yet efficient working barns. The circular floorplan of the building with its slatted upper floor allowed horses to tread over grain placed on the floor to break the heads from the stalks. The grain then fell through the slats into temporary storage below. The building seen today is a painstaking reconstruction of the original based on thorough research by numerous archeologists and curators.

Shipping and Receiving Dock

2 Shipping and Receiving Dock

The wharf of the plantation was the main transportation center for shipping outbound produce and receiving farming and household supplies. The Potomac River was a major carrier of passengers and trade goods in Washington's day. At this evocative spot on its banks, it is easy to imagine the bustle and excitement of early commerce on the Potomac River.

3 River Tours

Spirit Cruise Line: 1-866-404-8439, www.cruisetomountvernon.com ■ Potomac Riverboat Company: 703-684-0580, www.potomac-riverboatco.com
Visitors can still use the Potomac River to reach Mount Vernon. Two tour boat lines serve the wharf from the city: Spirit Cruise Line and Potomac Riverboat Company. Spirit Cruise Line also offers lovely summer river sightseeing tours originating and ending at Mount Vernon's wharf.

4 Slave Quarters

Many slaves had living spaces distributed over the plantation so that they were convenient to the work they were assigned. The remaining slaves lived communally in these quarters on the edge of the estate. In his will, Washington freed all his slaves and made provision for their ongoing support. Memorials to his slaves, erected in 1983, are located at the slave burial ground southwest of Washington's tomb, which itself is at the southwest end of the plantation.

5 Washington's Tomb
This tomb is the second to hold the remains of George and Martha Washington. It was erected in 1831 based on Washington's own instructions and, in the ensuing years, the tomb has been visited by millions of people who come to pay their respects the first US president.

6 Upper and Lower Gardens
The wonderfully colorful upper flower garden is densely planted with varieties known to be cultivated in Washington's time. The lower garden is surrounded by boxwood bushes that were planted before Washington's death. This orderly and expansive plot yielded a wealth of vegetables and berries for the plantation's kitchens.

7 The Greenhouse
The handsome greenhouse complex once helped protect exotic and valuable plants through the cold Virginian winter. Revolutionary-War-era visitors to Mount Vernon could enjoy English grapes, lemons, limes, and oranges, as well as a host of flowering tropical plants.

8 Museum
Over 500 artifacts offer an in-depth look at Washington's life and career from his early days as a surveyor to his post-presidency days at Mount Vernon. Among the items on display are his dress sword, his dentures, and his field bed from the Revolutionary War.

Gristmill and Distillery

9 Gristmill and Distillery
Open Apr–Oct: 10am–5pm daily ▪ Adm
Located 3 miles (5 km) from Mount Vernon on Route 235, South, is Washington's 18th-century watermill, which played an important part in his vision for America as a "granary to the world." Colonial millers grind wheat into flour and corn into meal just as was done in the 1700s. Archaeologists excavated the site of Washington's 1797 whiskey distillery, and a fully reconstructed distillery now provides demonstrations and hands-on activities.

10 Pioneer Farm
George Washington was passionate about improving the agricultural methods of his time. The Pioneer Farm showcases many new ideas and techniques he worked with, including a redesigned plow, crop rotation, and even organic farming. But families will most enjoy meeting the animals of the colonial farm, including Ossabaur Island pigs, Hog Island sheep, and Devon cattle.

Greenhouse and garden

The Top 10 of Everything

**The ornate Great Hall of the
Library of Congress**

🔟 Moments in History

Armies at the end of the Civil War on Pennsylvania Avenue in Washington, DC

1 Foundation of the Federal City

The US Constitution, ratified in 1788, provided and planned for "a District (not exceeding ten Miles square) as may, by Cession of Particular States..., become the Seat of the Government of the United States."

2 Layout and Design

In 1790, George Washington selected Pierre Charles L'Enfant, a French engineer, to lay out the city. The plan was influenced by Versailles and the city of Paris.

3 War of 1812

The United States declared war on Britain in 1812, seeking freedom of marine trade and the security of US seamen. In 1814, British troops entered the capital and burned government buildings, including the White House and the Capitol. If it had not rained, the whole city might have burned.

4 Expansion

Thomas Jefferson began western expansion by organizing the Lewis and Clark expedition in 1803. The C&O Canal and the Baltimore and Ohio Railroad provided a means of commerce through the mountains and launched a period of prosperity. New states were added to the Union, and bitter divisions arose connected to the issue of slavery.

5 Civil War

Conflict between the Union and the seceding Southern states began on April 12, 1861, plunging Washington and the nation into crisis. Union supporters, joined by thousands of blacks escaping slavery in the South, doubled the city's population in four years. Although threatened, the city was never taken by Confederate troops and, when the war ended in 1865, Washington was unharmed.

The burning of Washington, DC by the British in 1812

6 McMillan Plan

The McMillan Plan of 1901, so named for its congressional supporter, Senator James McMillan, was the first ever application of city planning in the US. It created much of the current layout of the Mall and President's Park.

7 New Deal

The Roosevelt era (1933–45) brought tremendous growth to the city. Efforts to bring the nation out of the Great Depression increased the size and number of government agencies, and provided direct funds for construction. Most of the buildings in the Federal Triangle, the completion of the Supreme Court, and the National Gallery of Art were New Deal works.

8 World War II

More than 10 percent of the US population of approximately 115 million was in uniform at the peak of the war, and the central management of all of these troops remained in Washington, DC.

Dr. Martin Luther King, Jr.

9 March on Washington

On August 28 1963, African-American leaders led 250,000 people to rally before the Lincoln Memorial in support of equal rights. Dr. Martin Luther King, Jr.'s eloquent dream for America, along with the size of the march, gave impetus to the struggle.

10 Home Rule

The federal government's control over the city was modified with the Home Rule Charter in 1973. This legislation gave the city power to elect its own mayor and council.

TOP 10 CITIZEN RIGHTS OF THE CONSTITUTION

United States Constitution

1 Inherent Rights
Freedom of religion, speech, the press, assembly, and seeking redress of citizen grievances.

2 Legality of Arms
The right of the people to keep and bear arms.

3 Quartering of Soldiers
Freedom from housing soldiers in private homes in peacetime and in war, except as prescribed by law.

4 Unjustified Searches
Freedom from unreasonable search and seizure of people, houses, and effects without a warrant.

5 Limits on Prosecutors
A grand jury indictment is required before trial; a person cannot be tried more than once for the same crime; a person cannot be forced to testify against himself; a person's property cannot be confiscated without compensation.

6 Protection of the Accused
Accused persons will be given a trial by a jury of peers, be informed of the charges, be able to confront witnesses, and be represented by counsel.

7 Civil Case Jury Trial
In common law, parties have a right to a trial by jury.

8 Unjust Punishment
The government cannot require excessive bail, impose excessive fines, or use cruel or unusual punishment.

9 Limited Scope
The stated rights do not limit other rights.

10 State Powers
All powers not granted to the US government belong to the states.

TOP10 US Presidents

George Washington

little doubt that the Federalist Papers, which he co-authored, helped gain its ratification.

5 Andrew Jackson
The success of Jackson (1829–37) as a leader in the Battle of New Orleans in 1814–15 made him a national hero. His popularity helped him win battles with Congress and with private business interests over issues such as banking and tariffs.

6 Abraham Lincoln
Unquestionably one of the greatest ever political leaders in any nation, Lincoln (1861–5) overcame inexpressible odds in preserving the Union and beginning the process of freeing slaves.

7 Theodore Roosevelt
The dawning of the 20th century brought an energetic and activist president to the helm. Roosevelt (1901–9) became famous for his military exploits in the Spanish–American War, but is best known for his opposition to business monopolies and pursuing a strong foreign policy. He also established the national parks system in the US.

1 George Washington
The United States' first president George Washington (1789–97) was never greater than when he refused to interpret the position of president as equivalent to "king."

2 John Adams
Adams (1797–1801) was among the young nation's most experienced diplomats, having managed affairs in Europe. He was the first US vice president, under Washington.

3 Thomas Jefferson
Jefferson (1801–9) is remembered for his embrace of democracy and his strong opposition to federal power.

John Adams

8 Woodrow Wilson
Wilson (1913–21) was a quiet academic who faced the greatest foreign task the nation had seen – participation in World War I. Wilson successfully set into place a legislative program that controlled unfair business practices, reduced tariffs, forbade child labor, and improved the banking system. He was awarded the Nobel Peace Prize in 1919.

4 James Madison
Madison (1809–17) demurred when he was called "the Father of the Constitution," stating that many minds had contributed, but there is

9 Franklin D. Roosevelt

Roosevelt's (1933–45) efforts to overcome the Great Depression never succeeded in the broadest sense, but they inculcated the federal government with a sense of respect for the rights and needs of the common man and the poorest of the poor. He led valiantly during World War II.

Franklin D. Roosevelt

10 John F. Kennedy

Kennedy (1961–3) brought an unprecedented style and flair to the presidency and can be credited with possibly the most important action of the 20th century – the prevention of nuclear war over Soviet missiles placed in Cuba. His assassination cut short his pursuit of a plan for progressive social programs, including more freedom and justice for African-Americans.

John F. Kennedy

TOP 10 FIRST LADIES

Hillary Clinton

1 Martha Washington
Martha established the role of the First Lady imitated by her successors. She was famous for accompanying George on military campaigns.

2 Dolley Madison
Dolley's social appeal greatly helped her slightly awkward husband.

3 Sarah Polk
The wife of James K. Polk (1845–9) was a strong force in the administration, writing speeches for the president.

4 Mary Todd Lincoln
Mary's pleasure at being First Lady was marred by the Civil War and her husband's assassination in 1865.

5 Grace Coolidge
The wife of Calvin Coolidge (1923–9) had a charm and tact that made her one of America's best-loved women.

6 Eleanor Roosevelt
Eleanor's interests were equal rights and social justice. She greatly increased the diplomatic role of the First Lady.

7 Jacqueline Kennedy
A stylish socialite, Jackie was an instant hit with the public and visiting diplomats.

8 Lady Bird Johnson
Wife of Lyndon B. Johnson (1963–9), her beautification projects had a direct impact on DC.

9 Hillary Clinton
The former First Lady (1993–2001) has gone on to be a Senator (2001–9), Secretary of State (2009–13) and presidential candidate for 2016.

10 Michelle Obama
A Harvard Law School graduate, she was a top lawyer, Chicago city administrator and community outreach worker before becoming the 44th First Lady.

TOP 10 Places of African-American History

1 Lincoln Memorial

This memorial touches the hearts of all African-Americans because of Abraham Lincoln's steadfastness in ending slavery in the US. It was here that Martin Luther King, Jr. made his "I Have a Dream" speech (see p45).

2 Martin Luther King, Jr. Memorial

MAP Q5 ▪ 1964 Independence Ave, SW ▪ Open 9am–10pm daily ▪ Dis. access

The Mall's first monument of an African-American, the Martin Luther King memorial commemorates the work of the Baptist minister, civil rights activist, and inspirational orator. The two massive stone tablets were designed by the Chinese sculptor Lei Yixin.

3 Metropolitan African Methodist Episcopal Church

MAP P3 ▪ 1518 M St, NW

This church was important in sheltering runaway slaves before the Civil War, and its pulpit has hosted many respected speakers, including Frederick Douglass, Martin Luther King, Jr., and Jesse Jackson. The funeral of civil-rights activist Rosa Parks was held here in 2005.

Martin Luther King, Jr. Memorial

4 Anacostia Museum and Center for African-American History and Culture

MAP E4 ▪ 1901 Fort Place, SE ▪ Open 10am–5pm daily ▪ Dis. access

This museum explores the role that African-Americans have played in the culture of the nation.

5 Cedar Hill

Frederick Douglass, a former slave, made many speeches for the rights of African-Americans, and was an adviser to Abraham Lincoln. He and his wife, Anna, moved into this Gothic-Italian-style house in 1877. In the garden is a humble stone hut nicknamed "The Growlery," which Douglass used as a study (see p49).

6 Mary McLeod Bethune Council House

A former cotton-picker, Bethune rose to be a leading educator of African-Americans and an activist for equal rights. Her home was headquarters

Mary McLeod Bethune Council House

of the National Council of Negro Women. She was also an adviser to Franklin D. Roosevelt *(see p45)*.

7 Mount Zion United Methodist Church

MAP L2 ■ 1334 29th St ■ 202-234-0148 ■ Services Sun 11am; open by appt at other times

Believed to be the first black congregation in the District, founded in 1816, Mount Zion's original building was an important stop on the Underground Railroad. Its present red-brick site was built in 1884. A small cottage holds a collection of artifacts reflecting the black history of Georgetown.

8 Lincoln Park

This pleasant urban park does justice to its dedication to Abraham Lincoln. The 1974 Robert Berks statue of Mary McLeod Bethune shows the great educator passing the tools of culture on to younger generations. The Emancipation Statue by Thomas Ball (1876) shows Lincoln holding his Proclamation in the presence of a slave escaping his chains *(see p82)*.

9 Frederick Douglass Museum

Another site associated with the statesman and abolitionist, this Capitol Hill townhouse was Douglass's home for nearly 10 years from the mid-1870s. Artifacts associated with Douglass are displayed here *(see p49)*.

Lincoln Park statue

10 National Museum of African-American History and Culture

MAP P5 ■ 1400 Constitution Ave, NW

The Smithsonian's newest museum opens in 2016, but the visitors' center is open already, with a photographic display of African-American history in its exhibition area.

TOP 10 AFRICAN-AMERICAN FIGURES

Marian Anderson

1 Ralph Bunche
The first African-American to receive the Nobel Peace Prize, because of his diplomatic efforts in the UN.

2 Duke Ellington
The musical genius was a native of Washington. He played his first paid performance on U Street.

3 Dr. Martin Luther King, Jr.
The charismatic leader of the civil rights movement.

4 Paul Lawrence Dunbar
Dunbar rose from poverty to gain recognition as a poet – the first African-American to do so – publishing his first collection in 1892.

5 Harriet Tubman
The best-known figure who freed slaves through the secret Underground Railroad network in the 19th century.

6 Ida B. Wells-Barnett
This celebrated crusader against anti-black government actions also marched in the 1913 women's suffrage rally.

7 Marian Anderson
In 1939, the singer was barred from Constitution Hall because of her race, so gave her Easter Sunday concert at the Lincoln Memorial instead.

8 Eleanor Holmes Norton
Norton has been effective as a non-voting House member, lobbying to promote Washington issues.

9 Walter E. Washington
Mayor of Washington from 1974 to 1978, the first elected mayor in the city for over 100 years.

10 Barack Obama
In November 2008, Obama was elected as the US's first African-American president.

🔟 Historic Homes and Buildings

1 Ford's Theatre

The theater where Lincoln was shot in 1865, has been restored by the federal government. It is now a memorial to the music- and theater-loving president (see p95).

2 Decatur House

MAP N3 ■ 1610 H Street, NW ■ 202-218-4338 ■ Open 10am–5pm Fri–Sat, noon–3:30pm Sun ■ Tours: 11am, 12:30pm & 2pm Mon, Wed & Fri

Stephen Decatur, a renowned naval hero, built this Federal-style town-house in 1818. It now houses the White House Historical Association, but has been preserved to evoke 19th-century middle-class America.

3 Gadsby's Tavern Museum

MAP D5 ■ 134 N Royal St, Alexandria, VA ■ 703-746-4262 ■ Open Apr–Oct: 10am–5pm Tue–Sat, 1–5pm Sun–Mon; Nov–Mar: 11am–4pm Wed–Sat, 1–4pm Sun ■ Adm

George Washington was a patron of this former tavern. The older of the two colonial buildings, dating from 1770, was a growing concern six years before the Declaration of Independence. The second building, the 1792 City Hotel, serves food typical of the 18th century.

Ford's Theatre facade

4 Carnegie Library

MAP Q3 ■ Mt Vernon Sq, NW

Philanthropist Andrew Carnegie's campaign to build libraries across America (he funded 1,679 in all) changed the country forever. This magnificent Beaux Arts building has been fully restored and is run by the Historical Society of Washington, DC.

5 Woodrow Wilson House

MAP M1 ■ 2340 S St, NW ■ 202-387-4062 ■ Open 10am–4pm Tue–Sun ■ Adm

The 28th president was exhausted and demoralized when he left office in 1921, but this Georgian Revival house must have done much to restore his spirits. It now gives a delightful insight into 1920s American life.

The drawing room of Woodrow Wilson House

6 Cedar Hill

MAP E4 ▪ 1411 W St, SE ▪ 202-426-5961 ▪ Open Apr 16–Oct 15: 9am–5pm daily (until 4:30pm Oct 16–Apr 15) ▪ Closed Thanksgiving, Dec 25, Jan 1 ▪ Dis. access ▪ Adm

Frederick Douglass and his wife Anna were the first African-American family in Anacostia when they moved to this house in 1877. Born a slave, Douglass became America's most effective anti-slavery speaker and writer (see p46).

7 Mary McLeod Bethune Council House

MAP P2 ▪ 1318 Vermont Ave, NW ▪ 202-673-2402 ▪ Open 9am–5pm daily

The renowned teacher (see p46) and advocate for women's and African-Americans' rights bought this Victorian townhouse – now a National Historic Site – in 1935. It is still furnished with her possessions.

Dumbarton Oaks

8 Dumbarton Oaks

This remarkable 1801 Federal-style home is filled with a Harvard-curated collection of Byzantine and pre-Columbian art. The house is surrounded by lovely gardens, with an orangery whose walls are draped in a 150-year-old ficus (see p105).

9 Old Stone House

The oldest surviving structure in DC, this evocative building holds demonstrations of crafts and skills of pre-Revolutionary life (see p107).

10 Sewall-Belmont House

Built in 1800, this enchanting home is one of the oldest on Capitol Hill. It is now a museum of women's emancipation (see p80).

TOP 10 ARCHITECTURAL SIGHTS

National Building Museum

1 National Building Museum
In this cavernous interior, displays examine architecture, engineering, design, and city planning (see p95).

2 Dwight D. Eisenhower Executive Office Building
The extravagant decoration is a favorite with architecture buffs (see p99).

3 Treasury Building
This 1836 Greek Revival building retains original features (see p100).

4 The Octagon
This building is now a museum of architecture and design (see p100).

5 Library of Congress
The most extensive library ever built contains exquisite decoration and more than 16 million books (see p79).

6 Old Post Office Pavilion
MAP P4 ▪ 1100 Pennsylvania Ave NW
This iconic Romanesque revival building was completed in 1899.

7 Pope-Leighey House
Alexandria, VA ▪ US 1 and Rte 235
The city's most innovative Frank Lloyd Wright design.

8 Supreme Court Building
This marble edifice never fails to delight (see p80).

9 Anderson House
MAP M2 ▪ 2118 Massachusetts Ave NW
This ornate Beaux Arts mansion, built in 1905 for Ambassador Lars Anderson, contains a spectacular 600-ft- (180-m-) long ballroom.

10 Cox's Row
MAP K2 ▪ 3327–29 N St NW
These Federal-style townhouses are outstanding examples of domestic architecture of the early 19th century.

🔟 Memorials and Monuments

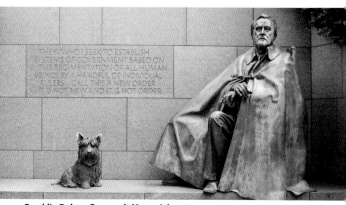

Franklin Delano Roosevelt Memorial

① Lincoln Memorial

The majestic monument to the president who preserved America's unity and began the long process of ending slavery is built in the form of a Greek temple. Daniel Chester French designed the enormous statue of a seated Abraham Lincoln in 1915, and it is among America's most inspiring sites, especially for its association with African-Americans' struggle for equality and opportunity *(see p86)*.

② Washington Monument

This spire is the dominant feature on the city skyline, 555 ft (170 m) high and clad in gleaming white marble. One of the tallest free-standing masonry constructions in the world, built between 1848 and 1884, it can be seen for miles *(see p87)*.

Vietnam Veterans Memorial

③ Jefferson Memorial

One of Jefferson's favorite Classical designs, the Pantheon in Rome, inspired this graceful monument. Dedicated in 1943 on the 200th anniversary of Jefferson's birth, it houses a 19-ft (6-m) bronze statue of the president by Rudolph Evans. It is especially enchanting when floodlit at night *(see p88)*.

④ Franklin Delano Roosevelt Memorial

This popular memorial, dedicated by President Clinton in 1997, has four outdoor "rooms," representing Roosevelt's four terms as president. Each is a composition of statues, water, plantings, and engraved quotations of the president. He is accompanied here, as in life, by his beloved Scottish terrier Fala, who rarely left his side. The memorial is a focus for activists for disabled citizens – Roosevelt was partially paralyzed by polio *(see p87)*.

⑤ Vietnam Veterans Memorial

This simple structure – a V-shaped black granite wall on which are carved the names of all those who died in this divisive war – has moved millions of visitors. The memorial, built in 1982, is the work of Maya Lin, who at the time was a 21-year-old architecture student at Yale *(see p86)*.

6 Korean War Veterans Memorial

Nineteen exhausted foot soldiers plod forward, determined on their goal. These 7-ft (2-m) steel statues are the dominant element in this memorial to the Americans who died in the UN's "police action" in Korea. A wall is etched with faces of actual soldiers. A circular pool invites quiet reflection *(see p88)*.

7 US Navy Memorial

The fountains that surround this plaza recirculate water from all the seven seas. Flagstaffs suggest the rigging of a tall ship *(see p96)*.

8 World War II Memorial

This memorial honors the 16 million who served in the US armed forces during World War II, but also the civilians who helped *(see p88)*.

9 African-American Civil War Memorial

MAP P1 ▪ 1000 U St, NW

"The Spirit of Freedom," a 1996 sculpture by Ed Hamilton, depicts African-American Union soldiers facing the enemy.

10 Iwo Jima Statue (Marine Corps Memorial)

MAP K5 ▪ 1400 N Meade St, Arlington, VA

Marines struggling to erect the Stars and Stripes on a ridge at Iwo Jima serves as a memorial to all marines who have fought for their country. The Pacific island saw fierce fighting, resulting in 7,000 American deaths, during World War II.

Iwo Jima Statue

TOP 10 STATUES

Abraham Lincoln Memorial

1 Abraham Lincoln
The marble vision of the president dominates Lincoln's memorial.

2 Neptune Fountain
Roland Hinton Perry created this grouping at the Library of Congress between 1897 and 1898 *(see p79)*.

3 Albert Einstein
MAP M4 ▪ 2101 Constitution Ave NW
This 1979 bronze by Robert Berks shows the great thinker in front of the National Academy of Sciences.

4 Benjamin Franklin
MAP P4 ▪ 1100 Pennsylvania Ave NW
Jacques Jouvenal's statue at the Old Post Office honors Franklin's creation of the US Postal Service.

5 First Division Monument
MAP N4 ▪ State Place & 17th St NW
A shining tribute to the First Infantry Division of World War I.

6 Andrew Jackson
MAP N3 ▪ Lafayette Sq, NW
This heroic equestrian statue was created by Clark Mills in 1853.

7 Winston Churchill
MAP H5 ▪ Massachusetts Ave NW
A 1966 sculpture by William M. McVey symbolizes the friendship between Britain and the US.

8 Ulysses S. Grant Memorial
This grouping took Henry Merwin Shrady 20 years to complete *(see p82)*.

9 Theodore Roosevelt
MAP L4 ▪ Roosevelt Island
Paul Manship's work shows the president gesticulating to his listeners.

10 Joan of Arc
MAP P1 ▪ Meridian Hill Park, Florida Ave & 16th St, NW
This 1922 work was a gift from the women of France to those of the US.

×REVOLUTIONARY·WAR·1775~1783× FREN

AL WAR 1798-1801 × TRIPOLI 1801-1805 × WAR OF 1812-1815 × FLORIDA·INDIAN WARS 1835-1842

🔟 Museums

A Douglas DC-3 aircraft on display at the National Air and Space Museum

① National Air and Space Museum

The 20th century's love affair with flight, from its intrepid beginnings to the mastery of space travel, is explored in this wonderful museum (see pp20–21).

② National Museum of American History

Mixing the "America's Attic" approach with fine contemporary interpretive exhibits, the museum offers visitors a fascinating look into America's past (see pp22–3).

Interior of the National Museum of the American Indian

③ National Museum of Natural History

Must-see exhibits abound here: the Dinosaur Hall (closed until 2019) will reveal one of the most complete T-Rex skeletons on reopening; the Hope diamond; the Insect Zoo; O. Orkin IMAX® theater; and a stunning mammal exhibit (see pp28–9).

④ National Museum of the American Indian

The Smithsonian's huge collection of material and artifacts related to Native American art, history, culture, and language moved into its first permanent home in Washington in 2004. Items include North American carvings, quilled hides, feathered bonnets, pottery, and contemporary artworks, as well as objects from Mexico, the Caribbean, and Central and South America (see p85).

⑤ United States Holocaust Memorial Museum

This ingeniously symbolic building houses documents tracing the Holocaust in Europe before and during World War II, grimly detailing the surveillance and the loss of individual rights faced by Jews, political objectors, gypsies, homosexuals, and

Previous pages Iwo Jima Statue (Marine Corps Memorial) at sunset

Children's artwork, United States Holocaust Memorial Museum

the handicapped. Moving eyewitness accounts, photographs, and artifacts all help to tell the story (see pp86–7).

6 National Postal Museum

Mail and fun don't naturally go together, but at this wonderfully conceived museum, they do. The little Pony Express saddlebags, tunnel-like construction represent- ing the desolate roads faced by the earliest mail carriers, and the mail- sorting railroad car all entertain and inform visitors (see p81).

7 International Spy Museum

This fascinating museum explores the role that spies have played in world events throughout history. The exhibitions tell the stories of individuals, reveal their missions and techniques, and display equipment.

8 National Archives of the United States

The Rotunda of the National Archives proudly displays the foundation documents of America: the Declaration of Independence, the Constitution of the United States, and the Bill of Rights. The museum features exciting interactive activities in the Public Vaults (see p88).

9 Newseum

This museum has an incredible collection of media coverage of events spanning the past five centuries. Significant moments in history such as the fall of the Berlin Wall and the 9/11 terrorist attacks have their own galleries (see p95).

10 Textile Museum

MAP M3 ■ 21st and G St, NW ■ See www. textilemuseum.org for opening times ■ Adm

Newseum

One of the world's foremost specialized museums reopened in a handsome new setting on George Washington University campus in fall 2014. It holds over 19,000 objects spanning 5,000 years, with fine collections of Peruvian, Pre-Columbian, Islamic, and Coptic textiles and Oriental carpets.

🔟 Art Galleries

Degas' *Dancers at the Barre*, in the Phillips Collection

1 National Gallery of Art

Displaying one of the most distinguished art collections in the world, this gallery gives visitors a broad but in-depth look at the development of American and European art over the centuries (see pp24–7).

2 The Phillips Collection

MAP M2 ▪ 1600 21st St, NW ▪ 202-387-2151 ▪ Open 10am–5pm Tue–Sat (to 8:30pm Thu); 11am–6pm Sun ▪ Adm ▪ Dis. access

Established in 1921, The Phillips Collection is America's first museum of modern art. It is celebrated for its Impressionist works, including Renoir's *Luncheon of the Boating Party*, Pierre Bonnard's *Open Window*, and Degas' *Dancers at the Barre*.

3 Corcoran Gallery of Art

Previously home to the Corcoran collection, this gallery now stages exhibits by the National Gallery of Art. The gallery is housed in one of America's most significant Beaux Arts buildings and was purchased by George Washington University in 2014. The site is also home to an art college (see p99).

4 Hirshhorn Museum and Sculpture Garden

The Hirshhorn exhibits the most varied modern and contemporary art in Washington, DC: its Directions gallery is known for displaying the newest – and sometimes the most controversial – work in the city. The lower level features a selection of recent additions to the collection, while large temporary shows are housed on the second floor, along with modern European sculpture. The third floor displays innovative paintings and sculptures up to the present day (see p85).

5 Renwick Gallery

Closed for major renovations until 2016, this gallery would be named by many Washingtonians as their favorite, not least because it is housed in a gorgeous French Renaissance-style building, as well as staging well-organized shows of American crafts. The Grand Salon, previously styled as a 19th-century picture gallery, was the subject of an international design competition to "re-envision" it as a contemporary exhibition space (see p99).

Hirshhorn Museum and Sculpture Garden

6 Freer Gallery of Art

MAP P5 ■ Jefferson Drive at 12th St, SW ■ 202-633-1000 ■ Closed for renovation until 2017 ■ Dis. access ■ www.asia.si.edu

The amazing Peacock Room is among the finest and most subtle examples of interior design found anywhere in the city. Created for a London home by James McNeill Whistler, and recreated here, the elegant painted walls and ceiling served as a complement to a collection of blue-and-white porcelain. The 19 galleries host art from Asia, as well as Far-East-influenced American art.

7 Arthur M. Sackler Gallery

MAP Q5 ■ 1050 Independence Ave, SW ■ 202-633-1000 ■ Open 10am–5:30pm daily; closed Dec 25 ■ Dis. access ■ www.asia.si.edu

Another of the underground museums of the Smithsonian, the Sackler is a leading center for the study and display of ancient and contemporary Asian art. Its events bring Asian art and philosophies to life, and its occasional presentations of Tibetan monks carrying out the ritual of sand-painting a mandala are always huge hits.

8 National Museum of African Art

This harmonious building brings architectural features common in Africa to one of the Smithsonian's most innovative museums, built principally underground. The wonderful permanent collection provides the best introduction to the role of art

Bronze statue of Shiva, Arthur M. Sackler Gallery

in African culture that one could hope to find (see p88). The pieces on display include ceramics, musical instruments, textiles, tools, masks, and figurines.

9 National Museum of Women in the Arts

This is the only museum in the world dedicated exclusively to displaying the work of women artists, from the Renaissance to the present day. Fascinating and provocative exhibitions explore the work and social role of female artists over the centuries, as well as that of women in general (see p96).

10 Kreeger Museum

MAP G5 ■ 2401 Foxhall Rd, NW ■ 202-337-3050 ■ Open 10am–4pm Sat; Tours 10:30am and 1:30pm Tue–Fri by appt only ■ Adm ■ Dis. access (main level and terrace)

This relatively unknown museum houses Impressionist works by 19th- and 20th-century painters and sculptors such as Rodin, Kandinsky, and Monet, as well as traditional works from Africa and Asia.

🔟 Off the Beaten Path

George Mason Memorial

1 George Mason Memorial
MAP N6 ■ www.nps.gov/gemm

George Mason, sometimes called the "forgotten Founding Father," was instrumental in framing the Constitution and creating the Bill of Rights. Located near the Jefferson Memorial, the Mason Memorial is a pleasant, open plaza with flower gardens and a fountain. A slightly larger-than-life statue of a smiling, seated Mason is popular with children, who climb into his lap to have their picture taken.

2 Kenilworth Aquatic Gardens

Laid out in 1882, these gardens feature numerous ponds filled with lotus and water lilies that bloom from late May to July. A trail through the surrounding Anacostia River marshlands makes this a fascinating stop for nature- and bird-lovers (see p61).

3 The Old Stone House
This charming blue granite Georgetown house dates from 1765, making it the oldest building in the Washington, DC area. In constant use as a shop or home until its

purchase by the government in 1953, it offers a fascinating look at what 18th-century life was like (see p107). Behind the vernacular house is an inviting Colonial Revival garden.

4 Lock-Keeper's House
MAP N4 ■ Corner of 17th Street and Constitution Ave, NW ■ Not open to the public

Looking out of place along modern Constitution Avenue, this small stone building offers a unique insight into DC's colorful past. In the 1800s, a branch of the C&O Canal ran where the avenue is today, and it was the keeper's job to operate the locks, raising and lowering passing barges, and to collect transit tolls.

5 National Postal Museum
This museum should be high on any visitor's list for the sheer fun it has relating the story of the American postal service. Historic biplanes hang from the high ceiling, while a real stagecoach is frozen in time, rushing mail to the wild west. Other exhibits include rare and unusual stamps, artifacts from the Pony Express, and even mail carried by Amelia Earhart on her famous transatlantic flight (see p81).

National Postal Museum

6 National Museum of Health and Medicine
MAP C2 ■ 2500 Linden Lane, Silver Spring, MD 20910 ■ 301-319-3300 ■ Open 10am–5:30pm daily ■ www.medicalmuseum.mil

Established by the US Army in 1862 to collect and study specimens for the advancement of Army medicine and surgery, this unique collection holds over 25 million fascinating (if somewhat morbid and not for everyone) items, including photos, historic medical artifacts, and preserved human remains. Exhibits include Civil

War-era bones and skulls showing battle wounds, and the bullet that killed President Abraham Lincoln.

7 Peirce Mill
MAP J4 ▪ **Tilden Street, NW** ▪ Open 10am–4pm Wed–Sun ▪ 202-895-6070 ▪ www.nps.gov/pimi/

This historic grist mill in Rock Creek Park *(see pp60–61)* was built in the 1820s and restored in the early 2000s. A tour of the mill offers a glimpse into DC's past, and you can enjoy a hike or picnic by sparkling Rock Creek. Demonstrations of the mill in action grinding grain are held every second and fourth Saturday.

8 Georgetown Waterfront Park
MAP L3

This pretty, tree-shaded park offers fine views of the busy Potomac from Lincoln Center to old Georgetown. Benches and a waterfront walkway make it a good place for relaxing, strolling, and picnicking.

9 National Geographic Museum
Anyone who has been thrilled by *National Geographic* magazine or TV documentaries will enjoy this small museum that showcases the famous photography of the magazine as well as constantly changing exhibits that highlight current stories and the work of the Society. Oddities abound, such as the 3D model of the Grand Canyon on the ceiling *(see p101).*

10 George Washington's Distillery
5513 Mount Vernon Memorial Hwy Alexandria, VA 22309 ▪ Open Apr–Oct: 10am–5pm daily ▪ www.mount vernon.org

George Washington's most successful business venture was making whisky. His distillery and grist mill, located about 3 miles (5 km) from the Mount Vernon estate, operate using methods and equipment typical of Washington's era. Entrance to the site is available only with a ticket to Mount Vernon *(see pp36–9).*

George Washington's Distillery

🔟 Green Spaces

The Smithsonian Castle presides over the Enid A. Haupt Garden

1 Enid A. Haupt Garden
These gardens sit on top of the Smithsonian Museums, and are inspired by the culture on display below. The Moongate Garden beside the Sackler Gallery reflects the Asian world, with its circular pool, pink granite, and cherry and beech trees. The Fountain Garden, alongside the Museum of African Art, evokes a Moorish ambience, with cascading waters and shaded seats.

2 US Botanic Garden
The gleaming glass-walled conservatory building is a beautiful home for this "living plant museum." Microclimates, such as desert, oasis, and jungle, reveal the variety and beauty of plant adaptations. Don't miss the primitive ferns and other plants dating back 150 million years.

Outside is the variegated National Garden with an environmental learning center (see p80).

3 Chesapeake and Ohio Canal
Canalboats on this 184-mile (295-km) 19th-century waterway carried cargo between Maryland and Georgetown for 100 years before the railroad put it out of business. The canal is now a National Historical Park, a haven for walkers, cyclists, canoeists, and boaters. Catch a mule-drawn boat ride at Georgetown or Great Falls (see p105).

4 National Arboretum
MAP E3 ■ 3501 New York Ave, NE ■ Open 8am–5pm daily ■ Dis. access

A world-acclaimed bonsai display – some trees are almost 400 years old – is one of the many collections that flourish on these 446 acres (180 ha). Azaleas, dogwoods, magnolias, herbs, roses, and boxwoods abound. A stand of columns, formerly on the US Capitol, adds a classical air.

5 Rock Creek Park
MAP J2 ■ 5200 Glover Rd NW ■ Open 9am–5pm Wed–Sun

This immense national park meanders with its namesake creek, offering something for everyone:

US Botanic Garden

Cherry trees at Dumbarton Oaks

woodland trails, 30 picnic areas, 25 tennis courts, a golf course, playing fields, and nature programs for kids and adults.

6 Dumbarton Oaks
Magnificent trees, including ancient oaks, soar above the park and gardens surrounding this historic Federal-style house. Designed by Beatrix Jones Farrand, the gardens range from formal to more casual settings. In spring, they are a mass of cherry blossom, and from March to October they are ablaze with wisteria, roses, lilies, and perennial borders. Pools and fountains tie the ensemble together (see p105).

7 Theodore Roosevelt Island
MAP L4 ■ George Washington Memorial Parkway ■ Open 6am–10pm daily ■ Dis. access
This wooded island on the Potomac River is the perfect memorial to the president who valued conservation. A 17-ft (5-m) statue of Roosevelt is the center-piece of what otherwise is a monument to nature – an unspoiled, idyllic space for birdwatching, hiking, fishing, and relaxing.

8 Bartholdi Park and Fountain
The French sculptor of the Statue of Liberty, Frédéric Auguste Bartholdi (1834–1904), also created this

Theodore Roosevelt statue

reflection of *belle époque* majesty. The 30-ft (9-m) sculpture's three caryatids support a circular basin surmounted by three tritons. A small garden surrounds the fountain like the setting for a gemstone (see p80).

9 East Potomac Park
MAP D4 ■ 14th St SW
One of Washington's best-kept secrets, this 300-acre (120-ha) peninsula has the Potomac River on one side and the boat-filled Washington Channel on the other. A paved walkway traces the waterfront, offering lovely views to runners, walkers, skaters, and fishermen. There is also a 9- and an 18-hole public golf course, and, in spring, thousands of cherry trees burst into pink blossom.

East Potomac Park

10 Kenilworth Park and Aquatic Gardens
MAP E3 ■ Gardens: 1550 Anacostia Ave, NE ■ Open 7am–4pm daily ■ Free ■ Dis. access ■ Park: Kenilworth & Burroughs Aves ■ Open 8am–dusk daily, closed Thanksgiving, Dec 25, Jan 1 ■ Dis. access
The lovely 14-acre (6-ha) Aquatic Gardens began as a hobby for Civil War veteran W.B. Shaw in 1882. He later transformed it into a commercial water garden. Now a National Park, the gardens are home to water lilies and lotuses, plus numerous varieties of birds, frogs, turtles, and butterflies. The adjacent Kenilworth Park offers acres of recreational areas and meadows.

🔟 Outdoor Activities

1 Boating

Thompson Boat Center: 2900 Virginia Ave, NW ▪ 202-333-9543 ▪ **Open Mar–Oct: 6am–8pm Mon–Sat, 7am–7pm Sun** ▪ **Washington Sailing Marina: 1 Marina Drive, Dangerfield Island, Alexandria, VA** ▪ 703-548-9027 ▪ **Open 9am–6pm daily**

Thompson Boat Center in Georgetown rents kayaks, rowing shells, canoes, and sailboats to reach Roosevelt Island and tour the waterfront. The Washington Sailing Marina rents sailboats for excursions on the Potomac. You should call in advance about certification requirements.

2 In-Line Skating
MAP C4

Rock Creek Park has been named one of the top 10 sites in the nation for in-line skating, but most bike trails allow skaters as well. You can rent skates and protective gear from one of the numerous in-line skating companies in the area.

3 Running

Runners and joggers are to be seen everywhere in Washington. The Mall is popular, as are the walkways around the Tidal Basin, Georgetown

Cycling by the US Capitol

Waterfront, the C&O Canal (see p60), East Potomac Park (see p61), and Rock Creek Park (see pp60–61).

4 Cycling

Bike and Roll: 901 G Street NW ▪ 202-842-2453 ▪ www.bikeandrolldc.com ▪ **Capital Bikeshare: www.capitalbikeshare.com**

Both Thompson Boat Center and the Washington Sailing Marina rent bicycles, and Capital Bikeshare has 175 stations in the city where you may use a credit card to rent a bike for a day or three days. Favorite routes are the C&O Canal towpath (see p60) and the Mount Vernon Trail (see pp36–9). Bike and Roll offers tours and rentals.

5 Golf

East Potomac Park: 972 Ohio Drive, SW (Hain's Point) ▪ **MAP J1** ▪ 202-882-7332 ▪ **Rock Creek Park Golf Course: 6100 16th St, NW** ▪ **MAP D4** ▪ 202-554-7660 ▪ **Langston Golf Course: 2600 Benning Rd, NE** ▪ **MAP E3** ▪ 202-397-8638

There are over 100 golf courses in the vicinity. Public golf courses include East Potomac Park and the Rock Creek Park Golf Course. Langston Golf Course,

Sailboats at Washington Harbour

located a few minutes from Capitol Hill, was among the first African-American courses in the US.

6 Hiking

The 4-mile (7-km) Western Ridge Trail and 5-mile (8-km) Valley Trail, both in Rock Creek Park *(see pp60–61)*, are scenic and gentle. The 11.5-mile (18.5-km) Capital Crescent Trail follows the old B&O Railroad route through Georgetown north to Bethesda. Trail information available at www.trails.com.

7 Informal Team Sports

Volleyball, dodge ball, rugby, softball, kickball, team Frisbee, and even polo are played on various fields at the western end of the Mall.

Kickball teams at play

8 Tennis

MAP D6 ▪ East Potomac Park Tennis Center: 1090 Ohio Drive, SW ▪ 202-554-5962

The East Potomac Park Tennis Center is operated by the National Park Service. Indoor and outdoor courts are available.

9 Horseback Riding

MAP J2 ▪ Rock Creek Horse Center: 5100 Glover Rd, NW ▪ 202-362-0117 ▪ Open noon–6pm Tue–Fri, 9am–5pm Sat & Sun

The Rock Creek Park Horse Center provides scheduled trail rides and riding lessons for all levels.

10 Climbing

860 Avery Lane, Rockville, MD ▪ 240-314-8643 ▪ www.rockvillemd. gov/climbinggym

The city of Rockville has a climbing gym in its Civic Center Park.

TOP 10 SPECTATOR SPORTS

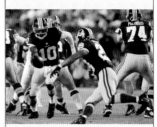

Washington Redskins

1 Washington Redskins
The National Football League Redskins are a year-round local obsession. Games are at FedEx Field in Maryland. Season tickets only.

2 Washington Wizards
The National Basketball Association team plays at the Verizon Center *(see p95)*. Buy tickets at the box office.

3 Washington Capitals
The National Hockey League team also plays its home games at the Verizon Center.

4 DC United
Robert F. Kennedy Stadium: 2400 E Capitol St, SE ▪ 202-547-9077
Robert F. Kennedy Memorial Stadium is home to professional soccer.

5 Baseball
Major league baseball at Nationals Park in DC, and Camden Yards in Baltimore.

6 Washington Mystics
The women's basketball professional league plays home games at the Verizon Center.

7 Citi Open
www.leggmasontennisclassic.com
This mid-summer tournament attracts major tennis pros.

8 Georgetown University Basketball
College Park, MD ▪ 202-397-Seat
Fast-paced action at the Verizon Center.

9 University of Maryland Athletics
ACC football and national basketball teams lead a varied program.

10 Naval Academy Football
The spectacle at these games is unmatched. Schedule and tickets: www.navysports.com

⑩ Children's Attractions

① National Air and Space Museum

Kids will be inspired by spectacular rockets and the 3D IMAX Journey Into Space, while their parents and grandparents can reminisce over the early days of aviation and space flight *(see pp20–21)*.

② National Zoological Park

The animals in Washington, DC's zoo are housed in large, recreated natural habitats and are close enough to be clearly observed. Sea lion demonstrations never fail to delight. The Speedwell Conservation Carousel showcases endangered species under a colorful open-air pavilion *(see pp32–3)*.

National Zoological Park

into several areas, including the Batman-themed Gotham City, Mardi Gras, and Coyote Creek. Younger children will adore Looney Tunes Movie Town. Hurricane Harbor is a huge water park with a dozen water-slides and a massive wave pool.

③ Six Flags America and Hurricane Harbor

13710 Central Avenue, Upper Marlboro, MD 20721 ▪ Open Six Flags: Apr–Sep: 10:30am–6–9pm (hours vary) daily; Oct: 5pm–midnight Fri, 10:30am–10pm Sat, 10:30am–9pm Sun ▪ Hurricane Harbor: May–Sep 11am–7pm daily (May: to 6pm Mon–Fri) ▪ Dis. access ▪ Adm ▪ www.sixflags.com/america

Children ready for a break from the memorials and monuments will love these parks. Six Flags features ten massive roller coasters with names like Ragin' Cajun and Mind Eraser, along with plenty of rides for smaller kids. The park is divided

④ The Capital Wheel at National Harbor

MAP D6 ▪ 165 Waterfront St, MD 20745 ▪ Open 4pm–10pm Mon–Fri, noon–10pm Sat & Sun ▪ Adm

The Capital Wheel at National Harbor lifts visitors 180 ft (55 m) above the ground in climate-controlled gondolas, offering fine views up and down the Potomac River from the National Mall to Mount Vernon.

⑤ Oxon Hill Farm

MAP D5 ▪ 6411 Oxon Hill Rd, MD 20745 ▪ Open 8am–4:30pm daily ▪ Closed Jan 1, Thanksgiving Day, Dec 25

Just a few miles from downtown DC, this working museum is a good place for kids to stretch their legs in the

Six Flags America roller coaster

great outdoors, while learning what rural farm life was like in the early 20th century. They can join in with activities such as feeding chickens, milking a cow, and riding around the farm on a hay wagon.

6 Wolftrap Children's Theater in the Woods

645 Trap Road, Vienna, VA 22182 ▪ Open late Jun–mid-Aug: see website for times ▪ Adm ▪ www.wolftrap.org
This endearing venue offers dance, music, puppetry, and plays for kids age 4 and up. The stage is down a pretty path in a woodland clearing. Most of the programs are interactive, encouraging kids to sing, dance, and get on stage with the performers.

7 Smithsonian Carousel

MAP P5 ▪ 900 Jefferson Drive, SW ▪ Open 10am–5pm daily ▪ Closed Dec 25 ▪ Adm

Smithsonian Carousel

In front of the Arts and Industries Building at the Smithsonian is a delightful, authentic carousel with brightly painted hand-carved animals. It only operates in good weather, but don't miss this bit of old-world fun if you have the chance. It also makes a refreshing break for kids starting to tire of the museums.

8 National Museum of Natural History

There is plenty here for young visitors, in particular the Insect Zoo featuring live specimens of giant hissing cockroaches and large leaf-cutter ants, and the Dinosaur Hall (closed until 2019) which contains a cast of a nest of dinosaur eggs and reconstructions of dinosaur skeletons. The Discovery Room allows children (and adults) to hold and touch objects such as crocodile heads and elephant tusks. The Live Butterfly Pavilion is home to exquisite species from around the world *(see pp28–9)*.

9 International Spy Museum

From a spy letter penned by George Washington, to James Bond's Aston Martin, this unique museum offers a kid-pleasing glimpse into the world of spies and espionage. The museum's thousands of artifacts include gadgets such as a German World War II Enigma machine, an umbrella that fires poison pellets, and a KGB lipstick gun.

International Spy Museum

Interactive activities allow kids to adopt disguises and undertake guided espionage activities. The Spy in the City Tour takes participants (10 and older) outside the museum, using a communications GPS to lead them through a simulated spy mission on the streets of DC *(see p96)*.

10 National Museum of American History

This kid-friendly museum has some great hands-on action for its younger visitors, including the Spark Lab where interactive exhibits explore the process of invention. Activities are targeted at children aged 6 to 12, but there is also the Under-5 Zone for younger kids. The award-winning Invention at Play area uses games and experiments to look at similarities between the way children and adults play, and the creative processes used by inventors *(see pp22–3)*.

National Museum of Natural History

Top 10 Theaters

Auditorium of the historic Ford's Theatre

1 Ford's Theatre

The tragedy of Abraham Lincoln's assassination here in 1865 kept this theater closed for over 100 years, but now it is the home of a vibrant theater company as well as being a museum, center for learning, and historic landmark (see p95).

2 Arena Stage

MAP Q6 ▪ 1101 6th St, SW
▪ 202-488-3300

Internationally renowned as a pioneering non-profit theater for over five decades, Arena has produced plenty of high-quality drama. The Arena reopened at Mead Center for American Theater in late 2010, making it the leading center for production, development, and study of American theater.

3 Folger Theatre

Visitors are treated to a rare experience in this Elizabethan-style Theatre, which strongly suggests the setting in which Shakespeare's works were originally performed. Works of the Bard and his near contemporaries are featured, and performances of medieval and baroque music fill the rich, varied schedule (see p79).

4 Shakespeare Theatre

MAP ▪ Q4 450 7th St, NW

Top actors, directors, designers, and lighting experts are involved in every dazzling production here. Although specializing in Shakespeare, the company also mounts works by other playwrights (see p79).

5 Kennedy Center

With works ranging from Shakespeare to Sondheim, from gripping drama and opera to light-hearted comedies and musicals, the many theater productions at this landmark arts center are almost always critically acclaimed. There are a variety of performance spaces catering to different styles, seating from just a few hundred people to more than 2,000 (see p99).

Kennedy Center

6 Woolly Mammoth Theatre Company

MAP Q4 ▪ 641 D St NW ▪ 202-393-3939

Widely acknowledged as Washington's most daring theater company, Woolly Mammoth stages new and innovative productions.

7 National Theatre

MAP P4 ▪ 1321 Pennsylvania Ave NW ▪ 202-628-6161

A wonderful venue that hosts top touring shows, the National Theatre opened in 1835. Since then, every US president has attended at least one of its performances. Many Broadway classics have staged their premiere here, including *Showboat* and *West Side Story*.

National Theatre

8 Gala Hispanic Theatre

MAP D3 ▪ 3333 14th St, NW

The recipient of a huge number of awards, this theater mounts works in Spanish with simultaneous English translation. Brilliant productions of works from the classical to the absurd attract a diverse audience.

9 Studio Theatre

MAP P2 ▪ 1501 14th St, NW

Off-Broadway hits, classics, and experimental fare make up the season at this performance landmark with two theater spaces.

10 Harman Center for the Arts

MAP Q4 ▪ 610 F St, NW

The Harman Center is an 21st-century expanded stage for the Shakespeare Theatre Company, as well as offering great theater, ballet, and musical performances.

TOP 10 ENTERTAINMENT VENUES

Lisner Auditorium event

1 Verizon Center
The home of DC's basketball and hockey teams has many attractions beyond the games *(see p95)*.

2 Warner Theatre
MAP P4 ▪ 13th & E Sts, NW
You'll find Broadway shows, comedians, and concerts here.

3 Carter Barron Amphitheatre
MAP D2 ▪ 4850 Colorado Ave, NW
Open-air stage in Rock Creek Park. Shows throughout summer *(see p72)*.

4 Coolidge Auditorium
MAP S5 ▪ Library of Congress, 10 1st St, SE
The home of the Library of Congress music series *(see p79)*.

5 Lisner Auditorium
MAP M3 ▪ 21st and H Sts, NW
This university theater features everything from world music to classical orchestras.

6 Nationals Park
MAP E4 ▪ 1500 S Capitol St, SE
Home to the Nationals Baseball team, this park is the city's latest highlight.

7 DAR Constitution Hall
MAP N4 ▪ 1776 D St, NW ▪ Dis. access
The largest concert hall in DC.

8 Lincoln Theatre
MAP P1 ▪ 1215 U St, NW
An intimate setting for jazz, soul, and gospel music.

9 Wolf Trap
Metro West Falls Church ▪ 1551 Trap Rd, Vienna, VA
An open-air venue for big names in entertainment.

10 Jiffy Lube Live
7800 Cellar Door Drive, Bristow, VA ▪ Rte I-66 to exit 44
International rock stars perform at this open-air arena.

🔟 Restaurants

① Central Michel Richard
MAP P4 ▪ 1001 Pennsylvania Ave, NW ▪ $$

Sizeable plates of comfort food, such as braised lamb shanks with *spaetzel*.

② Blue Duck Tavern
Traditional American fare is served in a contemporary neighborhood tavern *(see p103)*.

West End Bistro

③ West End Bistro
MAP M3 ▪ 1190 22nd St, NW ▪ $$

Located in the Ritz-Carlton, this bistro adds European accents to fine American ingredients.

④ Acadiana
MAP Q3 ▪ 901 New York Ave, NW ▪ $$$

This elegant restaurant offers modern interpretations of Louisiana dishes by chef Jeff Tunks.

⑤ Obelisk
MAP N2 ▪ 2029 P St, NW ▪ $$$

Obelisk serves a fixed-price menu of the finest Italian dishes.

⑥ Nora
MAP R2 ▪ 2132 Florida Ave, NW ▪ $$$

Refined, inspired New American cuisine is created from organically grown ingredients.

⑦ Komi
MAP N2 ▪ 1509 17th St, NW ▪ 202-332-9200 ▪ $$$

Reserve well in advance at this much-fêted temple to modern Greek cuisine.

⑧ Marcel's
MAP M3 ▪ 2401 Pennsylvania Ave, NW ▪ $$$

Classic french cuisine. Diners can choose one of four *prix-fixe* dinners ranging from four to seven courses.

⑨ Vidalia
MAP N3 ▪ 1990 M St, NW ▪ 202-659-1990 ▪ $$$

Southern charm meets European elegance in this acclaimed restaurant.

⑩ 1789
Federal-style townhouse serving a medley of lamb, oysters, and other dishes *(see p109)*.

For a key to restaurant price ranges see p83

🔟 Shopping

① The Fashion Centre at Pentagon City
MAP C4 ▪ 1100 S Hayes St

Nordstrom and Macy's are the two anchors here, plus over 170 other stores, a food court, and a spa.

② National Harbour
MAP D6 ▪ Rte I-295 S

On the shores of the Potomac River, and with over 150 retailers, this is one of DC's hottest shopping venues.

③ Friendship Heights
MAP G2

Home to some of the most exclusive retail outlets in DC. Mazza Gallerie is a small, upscale mall and other stores include Tiffany, Dior, and Cartier.

④ Potomac Mills Mall
2700 Potomac Mills Circle 307, Woodbridge, VA

This is one of the largest discount malls in the world.

⑤ The Shops at National Place
MAP P4 ▪ 529 W 14th St, NW

The shops here are mainly specialty boutiques and small emporiums.

⑥ Eastern Market
This market is an appetizing source of picnic provisions on weekdays and a carnival of arts and crafts vendors on weekends (see p81).

Georgetown store

⑦ Tysons Corner Center and Galleria at Tysons II
1961 Chain Bridge Rd, McLean, VA & 2001 International Drive, McLean, VA

This huge two-site shopping complex features Nordstrom, Bloomingdale's, Lord & Taylor, Saks Fifth Avenue, Macy's, and Neiman Marcus.

⑧ Penn Quarter
7th and G Street ▪ MAP Q4

This district is filled with restaurants, stores such as Bed, Bath & Beyond and Aveda, and small boutiques.

⑨ Georgetown
MAP L2

Probably the most famous shopping area in the city, partly because of the hundreds of shops, but also for the pervasive sense of style.

⑩ 14th and P Street
MAP P2

This gentrified area is filled with galleries, restaurants, boutiques, and stores, especially furniture shops.

Potomac Mills Mall illuminated in the evening light

🔟 Washington, DC for Free

Lionesses basking in the sun at the National Zoological Park

① Animal Magic

One of the best free places to spend a day outdoors is the National Zoological Park. There are all the usual animals but one of the biggest draws is the Giant Pandas: Mei Xiang, Tian Tian, and the recent cute cub, Bao Bao (see pp32–3).

② Architectural Gems

Washington's superlative architecture is all around you, but is typified by three remarkable buildings: the National Archives (see p88); the Library of Congress Jefferson Building (see p79), and Union Station (see p79). You can see the first two on a free guided tour; Union Station is open to all.

Union Station splendor

③ Children's Theater

The National Theatre offers free kid-oriented Saturday morning entertainment at 9:30am and 11am – tickets are issued 30 minutes beforehand. Shows range from short plays such as Snow White and the Seven Dwarves, to magic, puppetry, and music of all sorts (see p67).

④ Lunchtime Music

MAP P4 ■ www.itcdc.com/visitor-information/entertainment/live!-on-woodrow-wilson-plaza.aspx
All summer long, some of the DC's best toe-tapping free music can be found at lunchtime in the Woodrow Wilson Plaza at the Ronald Reagan Building. Pack a picnic lunch or visit the adjacent food court for supplies.

⑤ Capitol Walking Tour

One of the best freebies in town is the walking tour of the US Capitol building. It melds art and architecture, every element of which celebrates the vision of America's Founding Fathers (see pp12–13).

⑥ Culture at the Kennedy

The Kennedy Center offers a free performance on the Millennium Stage every day at 6pm. Offerings range from music to dance, poetry, comedy, and theater (see p99).

7 Free Flicks
MAP P5 ■ www.dcoutdoorfilms.com

During the summer months, Screen on the Green brings free movies to a giant screen on the National Mall near the Washington Monument. Other outdoor cinema locations include Capitol Hill and Georgetown Waterfront Park. Bring a blanket and snacks (no alcohol) and enjoy the show.

8 Green Escape
The United States Botanical Garden offers a lush, free refuge to Mall-weary visitors. The vast and beautiful conservatory shelters over 4,000 varieties of plants from around the world. Favorite exhibits include the Jungle, the Orchid Collection, and the Children's Garden (see p80).

9 Priceless Plantings
At the 640-acre (260-ha) National Arboretum, walkers and cyclists are free to explore the myriad paths leading to such delights as a hidden pagoda in the Japanese Stroll Garden. From mid-April to May, tens of thousands of azaleas are in bloom (see p60).

National Arboretum

10 Making Money for Free
MAP P5 ■ 14th and C Sts
■ 202-874-2330 ■ Open 8:30am–3:30pm Mon–Fri ■ Dis. access
■ www.moneyfactory.gov/tours.html

One of DC's most popular tours is that of the Bureau of Engraving and Printing, where visitors can goggle at millions of US dollars being printed. Tickets are required from March to August: be at the ticket booth at 8am to be sure of a ticket for that day.

MONEY-SAVING TIPS

Washington, DC Metrorail station

1 DC street vendors can be pricey. For a low-cost alternative, hit the food court in Union Station (see p79), or the Cafeteria at the Capitol Visitor Center (see p13). Better yet, pack a lunch and enjoy it on the Mall.

2 Free Tours by Foot offers walking tours in various DC locations. Not exactly free, at the end of the tour you are asked to make a donation. www.freetoursbyfoot.com

3 The Metrorail is fast, efficient, and affordable. Fares are higher during rush hour, so try to time travels for the middle of the day and the evening.

4 Plan your trip to cover a weekend. On weekends hotel room rates can be as little as half the weekday rates.

5 Look for a hotel that offers a robust free breakfast. It saves you time and the cost of a meal.

6 If you have a car with you, buy your gas outside DC, where it is usually much cheaper.

7 Hotels are also often cheaper in nearby Virginia and Maryland.

8 Check online private rental sites like VRBO (vrbo.com) and Airbnb (airbnb.com). It is possible to find a quality apartment or condominium in a great neighborhood for the about the same price as a discount hotel room.

9 TicketPlace sells half-price tickets to a variety of theater, dance and musical performances throughout the city. culturecapital.tix.com

10 Check websites and call those attractions that charge admission. They often offer discounts at specific times, or give out coupons that lower admission fees.

🔟 Festivals and Cultural Events

1 Smithsonian Folklife Festival

Fascinating and entertaining cookery, storytelling, craft-making, dancing, music, and art fill the National Mall for two weeks around Independence Day (July 4). This is undoubtedly one of the largest and best cultural events in the world.

2 Shakespeare Free for All

MAP Q4 ■ 610 F St, NW ■ www.shakespearetheatre.org

The first two weeks of June bring free performances by the Shakespeare Theatre Company (see p66) at the Sidney Harman Hall. Tickets are made available by online lottery and at the venue on the day.

Folklife Festival

3 National Cherry Blossom Festival

Late Mar–mid-Apr

The Tidal Basin is surrounded by beautiful Japanese cherry trees, which originated with the gift of 3,000 specimens to the city in 1912 by the mayor of Tokyo. The festival celebrating their spring blossoming includes a parade, performances, and such offbeat but appropriate events as a sushi-making contest.

National Cherry Blossom Festival

4 National Capitol Barbecue Battle

MAP P4 ■ www.bbqindc.com ■ Late Jun

Pennsylvania Avenue is awash with the enticing smell of smoked pork during the annual National Capitol Barbecue Battle. Top barbecue restaurants and pit-masters from around DC and the nation gather to compete for $40,000 in prize money. Visitors get to stroll the five-block-long venue, sampling tasty dishes, enjoying music, cooking demonstrations, and children's activities.

5 Capital Jazz Festival

Merriweather Pavilion, Columbia, MD ■ www.capitaljazzfest.com ■ Early Jun

This annual three-day festival of jazz and blues boasts an impressive line-up of national and international artists and bands.

6 Washington National Cathedral Christmas Services

In early December, the cathedral (see pp30–31) inaugurates the Christmas season with an open house featuring bagpipes, group singing, pageantry, and stunning seasonal decorations. Then, throughout the season, music and concerts are presented, culminating with the elaborate celebrations of Christmas Eve and Christmas Day.

Filmfest DC
www.filmfestdc.org

This top-quality and lively festival of movies has brought the best of world cinema to the city since 1986. The most exciting new films are shown during two weeks in April at various venues, and discussions and film-oriented events are held at theaters, auditoriums, and cafés across town.

8 National Book Festival
www.loc.gov/bookfest

Organized and sponsored by the Library of Congress, this festival takes place on a day in September at the Washington Convention Center and is free and open to the public. Around 50 authors of fiction, non-fiction, and children's books give readings, presentations, interviews, and book signings; plus, there are giveaways, promotions, and activities sponsored by a number of leading publishing companies.

National Book Festival

9 Washington Nationals
MAP E4 ■ 1500 S Capitol St, SE
■ 888-632-NATS ■ www.nationals.com

Big-league baseball returned to Washington in 2005 after a 30-year absence. The Washington Nationals fill the stands of the Nationals Park from April to October.

10 Chinese New Year
Late Jan–early Feb

New Year is celebrated on a Sunday with a parade, fireworks, special menus at the restaurants, and traditional events in Chinatown. Simply pass through the ornate arch at 7th and H streets, NW to join in the colorful festivities.

TOP 10 ONE-DAY EVENTS

Smithsonian Kite Festival

1 Smithsonian Kite Festival
National Mall ■ Late Mar–early Apr
Competitions include home-built kites, fighting kites, and others.

2 Independence Day
National Mall ■ Jul 4
The celebration culminates with a fireworks display synchronized with patriotic music.

3 White House Easter Egg Roll
Easter Mon
Children's activities, music, and egg rolling. Advance tickets only.

4 National Christmas Tree Lighting
The Ellipse ■ Early Dec
The decorations are joyous.

5 National Frisbee Festival
Washington Monument ■ Late Aug
The Frisbee dogs always steal the show.

6 Memorial Day
Last Mon in May
Concerts, ceremonies, and a parade along Constitution Avenue honor those who have died in the service of their country.

7 National Symphony Labor Day Concert
US Capitol ■ Labor Day
The official end of summer.

8 International Gold Cup Steeplechase Races
Great Meadows Events Centers, The Plains, VA ■ Mid-Oct
Take place at the peak of fall's colored foliage.

9 St. Patrick's Day
Sun before Mar 17
A parade on Constitution Ave, SE.

10 Martin Luther King, Jr. Day
3rd Mon in Jan
Church services held. Check local papers for details.

⟨TOP 10⟩ Trips from Washington, DC

Fall colors on Skyline Drive, Virginia

① Annapolis, Maryland
Rte 50 ▪ William Paca House: 186 Prince George St; Open 10am–5pm Mon–Sat, noon–5pm Sun; Closed Dec–Mar ▪ Adm

This enticing city on the Chesapeake Bay is one of the great sailing centers on the East Coast as well as being home to the US Naval Academy. The 18th-century home of William Paca, the governor who signed the Declaration of Independence, is here. Tours of the State Capitol are also popular.

② Harpers Ferry, West Virginia
Rte 340

Before the Civil War, John Brown carried out his famous raid against government troops here, protesting the legality of slavery in the United States. This picturesque little town around the old Potomac waterfront has been well preserved and is filled with exhibits about its history.

Annapolis, Maryland

③ Skyline Drive, Virginia
Off Rte I-66

This delightful winding road passes 107 miles (170 km) through the mountain and valley scenery of Virginia's Shenandoah National Park. Many hiking trails to isolated peaks, waterfalls, and rare forest environments begin from the main highway.

④ Baltimore, Maryland
Rte I-95

Called "Charm City" by its residents and promoters, Baltimore offers museums of art, industry, baseball, science, railroads, and marine trade along with historic sites from every American period. Its phenomenal National Aquarium is among the finest in the world. The historic Lexington Market, established in 1782, is still going strong with over 140 food vendors.

⑤ Chincoteague and Assateague, Virginia
Off Rte 13

Assateague Island is famed for its wild ponies. The pony swim and auction, held on the last Wednesday and Thursday of July, is a major tourist attraction. The Chincoteague National Wildlife Refuge is a paradise for bird-watchers and nature buffs. The local seafood is first-rate, and the ice cream made here is justifiably famous.

6 Colonial Williamsburg and Historic Jamestown
Off Rte 1-95 S

Williamsburg was the capital of the fledgling United States during the Revolutionary War. Today, Colonial Williamsburg is the largest living history museum in America, with over 500 reconstructed colonial buildings. Nearby, Jamestown is a reconstruction of the first successful English settlement in America.

Colonial Williamsburg

7 Fredericksburg, Virginia
Rte 1

This city on the Rappahannock River offers colonial homes, moving Civil War sites, and a downtown filled with shops and restaurants. A marked walking tour lays out milestones in the city's history.

8 Frederick, Maryland
Rte I-270

Noted for its majestic bridges, Frederick is a city that is steeped in the memory of 19th-century life and Civil War battles. The city also has an exceptional artistic and cultural life.

Gettysburg statue

9 Manassas Battlefield
Off Rte I-66

This Civil War battlefield is where Confederate and Union soldiers fell by the thousands fighting for conflicting visions of the nation's future. Manassas experienced two pitched battles, the first an opening confrontation of untested troops, the second a bloodbath.

10 Gettysburg, Pennsylvania
Rte 15

The three-day battle of Gettysburg in 1863 was the bloodiest of the Civil War, killing over 51,000. Lincoln famously dedicated the cemetery here. The Gettysburg National Military Park is among the most visited sites on the East Coast.

Washington, DC
Area by Area

Colorful townhouses in Georgetown

🔟 Around Capitol Hill

Buzzing with the business of government, Capitol Hill is also a place for shopping, entertainment, food and drink, or simply strolling its handsome neighborhood streets. Approached from the west, the area begins with the meticulously land-scaped US Capitol complex, which, as well as the Capitol itself, includes the US Botanic Garden, the Supreme Court

Folger Shakespeare Library and Theatre

Building, and the Library of Congress. Union Station, to the north, is one of the finest railroad terminals in the world.

AROUND CAPITOL HILL

1 US Capitol

Symbolizing both government power and the control of that power by the people, the Capitol crowns the east end of the Mall *(see pp12–15)*.

2 Folger Shakespeare Library and Theatre

MAP S5 ▪ 201 East Capitol St, SE ▪ 202-544-4623 ▪ Open 10am–5pm Mon–Sat ▪ Dis. access

The Folger has the world's largest library of printed editions of Shakespeare's works, and performances at the 16th-century-style theater give viewers an insight into Shakespeare and his times. There is also a huge

Union Station's magnificent interior

supporting collection of Renaissance works in other fields, as well as playbills, musical instruments, and costumes. The elegant Neo-Classical building, a 1929 design by Paul Philippe Cret, is on the National Register of Historic Places *(see p66)*.

3 Union Station

MAP R4 ▪ 50 Massachusetts Ave, NE ▪ Dis. access

Opened in 1907, this magnificent Beaux Arts building is still a fully functional transportation hub. The lofty barrel-vaulted concourse, decorated with 70 lbs (32 kg) of gleaming gold leaf, is one of the great public spaces in the city – the Washington Monument, laid on its side, would easily fit within its length. Over 23 million people pass through the station each year.

4 Library of Congress

MAP S5 ▪ 101 Independence Ave, SE ▪ 202-707-5000 ▪ see website for visiting times ▪ Dis. access

The largest collection of books, recordings, and images in the world got its humble start when the US government bought 6,487 books from Thomas Jefferson after the first congressional library was destroyed by fire in 1814. Free hour-long tours of the spectacular Jefferson Building include stops at the remarkable Italianate-pillared Great Hall; the vast, circular Main Reading Room; a rare Gutenberg Bible; and Thomas Jefferson's original book collection.

0 meters 400
0 yards 400

STREET NE

STREET NE

MARYLAND AVENUE NE

E STREET NE

D STREET NE

C STREET NE

CONSTITUTION AVENUE NE

NORTH CAROLINA AVENUE NE

8TH 9TH 10TH 11TH 12TH 14TH STREET

④ Lincoln Park ⑤

NORTH CAROLINA AVENUE SE

SE AVENUE

SE

8TH 9TH 10TH 11TH 12TH 13TH 14TH STREET

G ST SE

1 **Top 10 Sights** see pp79–81

① **Places to Eat** see p83

① **The Best of the Rest** see p82

5 Supreme Court Building

MAP S4 ■ 1st St and East Capitol St, NE ■ 202-479-3211 ■ Open 9am–4:30pm Mon–Fri except federal holidays ■ Dis. access

The home of the highest seat of the judicial branch of the US government is a handsome Neo-Classical building designed by Cass Gilbert – the architect who designed the beautiful Woolworth Building in New York City – and completed in 1935. On its west pediment, above the marble columns of the main entrance, is inscribed in bold letters the famous motto "Equal Justice Under Law."

6 US Botanic Garden

MAP R5 ■ On the Capitol grounds at Maryland Ave and 1st St, SW ■ 202-225-8333 ■ Open 10am–5pm daily ■ Dis. access

Long valued by Capitol Hill residents as a quiet retreat, the Botanic Garden Conservatory is home to some 4,000 living plants that have been arranged into themes and biosystems, such as Plant Exploration, Jungle, Oasis, and Medicinal Plants. The wedge-shaped National Garden, situated to the west of the Conservatory, includes glorious colorful outdoor displays. The main court is a wonderfully fragrant spot and a perfect place to sit and rest, and there's a Children's Garden to keep youngsters happy *(see p60)*.

CAPITOL HILL RESIDENCES

In the early 19th century, the area east of the Capitol was filled with a motley collection of boarding houses and taverns where members of Congress stayed during legislative sessions. During the 19th and into the 20th centuries, a diverse mix of housing styles – Federal townhouses, manor houses, Queen Anne, interspersed with two-storey frame dwellings – developed. The protected Capitol Hill Historic District is now the largest historic residential district in the city.

7 Bartholdi Park and Fountain

MAP R5 ■ 1st St & Washington Ave, SW ■ Dis. access

Another oasis for Capitol Hill visitors, this immaculate park is bursting with flowers and ornamental plants. Its symmetrical design radiates out from the fine Gilded Age cast-iron Bartholdi Fountain, a three-storey-high construction of supple human forms, European-style lights, and a non-stop flow of water *(see p61)*.

8 Sewall-Belmont House

MAP S4 ■ 144 Constitution Ave, NE ■ 202-546-1210 ■ Tours noon–4pm Wed–Sun ■ Donation

Built in 1750 and expanded in 1800, this house is one of the most historic in Washington. It was the only private

Bartholdi Park and Fountain

Stalls at the Eastern Market

residence burned during the War of 1812 because only from here did Americans fire on the invading British (see p42). The completely rebuilt house was bought by the National Women's Party in 1929 and remains their home today. Visitors can see the elaborate but homely period furnishings, as well as objects and documents fundamental to the suffragist and feminist movements in the United States, and the country's oldest feminist library (see p49).

(9) Eastern Market
MAP S5 ▪ 7th St & C Street, SE

Completed in 1873, Eastern Market has been a key element in Capitol Hill's history. Designed by a prominent local architect, Adolph Cluss, it symbolized the urbanization of the city at the end of the Civil War. Since then, it has served as a neighborhood meeting place for residents, and as a focal point in the area's revitalization. Following a fire in 2007, restoration has repaired the building's distinctive architecture.

(10) National Postal Museum
MAP R4 ▪ 12 Massachusetts Ave, NE ▪ Open 10am–5:30pm daily ▪ Dis. access

The US Postal Service delivers over 600 million items of mail every day, and this fun museum traces its development from the days of the Pony Express onwards (see p58).

A DAY AROUND EASTERN MARKET

Library of Congress

Folger Shakespeare Library and Theatre

The Market Lunch Eastern Market

The Flea Market at Eastern Market

Woven History and Silk Road

Eastern Market Metro Station

▶ MORNING

Before a day of shopping, begin with a bit of history at the **Library of Congress** (see p79), a handsome example of the Italian Renaissance style, with unsurpassed interiors. The first tour is at 10:30am.

Turn right onto East Capitol Street, then right again, and continue one block to the **Folger Shakespeare Library and Theatre** (see p79). The Elizabethan theater is enchanting, and the materials on display are both rare and fascinating, as are the changing temporary exhibitions.

Walk east to 7th Street and turn right. A little over two blocks farther on is **Eastern Market**. On weekends, it is surrounded by arts and crafts vendors and flower stalls. **The Market Lunch** (see p83) inside is a great choice for a bite to eat and a rest.

AFTERNOON

If it's a Sunday, spend the afternoon at **The Flea Market at Eastern Market**, on 7th Street between C and Pennsylvania. It features 100 or more vendors selling antiques, Oriental rugs, fabrics, fine art photographs, jewelry, and other items. If the flea market is closed, walk a block south of Eastern Market and visit **Woven History and Silk Road** (311–5 7th St, SE; 202-543-1705; Open 10am–6pm daily) for its fabrics, rugs, and crafts from Asia and South America.

To return home, turn right and the **Eastern Market Metro Station** is straight ahead of you.

See map on pp78–9

The Best of the Rest

1 Capital Grounds
MAP R4–5

The lovely gardens and walkways that surround the Capitol are the work of renowned landscape designer Frederick Law Olmsted, who created the plan for the grounds in 1874.

2 Ebenezer United Methodist Church
MAP S5 ▪ 420 D St, SE ▪ Open 10am–2pm Mon–Fri

The first congregation of African-American Methodists and Episcopals in Washington. It also became home to the first public school for black children after the Emancipation Proclamation.

3 Alleys and Carriageways
MAP S5

The alleys of Capitol Hill, notorious in the 19th century for their squalid and cramped residences, have today been turned into charming little homes.

4 Emancipation Monument
Lincoln Park ▪ Metro Eastern Market

Lincoln holds the Emancipation Proclamation while the last slave, Archer Alexander, breaks his chains (see p47).

5 Statue of Mary McLeod Bethune
Lincoln Park ▪ Metro Eastern Market

This modern sculpture shows the great African-American educator and activist with two African-American children. It symbolizes knowledge handed down through generations (see p46).

6 Frederick Douglass Museum
MAP S4 ▪ 320 A St, NE ▪ Open 9am–4pm daily, by appt. only ▪ 202-544-6130

The home of the African-American activist contains many of his possessions, including a document proclaiming him a "freed man" (see p49).

7 Christ Church
MAP S6 ▪ 620 G St, SE

This elegant church, built in 1805, had many prominent parishioners, including presidents Jefferson, Madison, and Monroe.

8 National Guard Memorial Museum
MAP R4 ▪ 1 Massachusetts Ave, NW ▪ 202-408-5887 ▪ Open 9am–4pm Mon–Fri ▪ Dis. access

This gallery remembers citizens who gave their lives to protect the nation.

9 American Veterans Disabled for Life Memorial
MAP R5 ▪ 150 Washington Ave, SW

This lovely plaza-like oasis is one of DC's newest memorials. It features a tree-shaded, star-shaped pool and interpretive glass and bronze panels.

10 Ulysses S. Grant Memorial
US Capitol ▪ MAP R5

This equestrian grouping honors the Union victory in the Civil War. Sculptor Henry Shrady (1871–1922) took 20 years to complete the work (see p51).

Ulysses S. Grant Memorial

Places to Eat

PRICE CATEGORIES

For a three-course meal for one with half a bottle of wine (or equivalent meal), taxes and extra charges.

$ under $50 $$ $50–100 $$$ over $100

A table at The Monocle

 Dubliner Pub
MAP R4 ▪ 4 F Street ▪ 202-737-3773 ▪ Dis. access ▪ $

An Irish pub with free-flowing pints and good hearty food. Try the lamb with mustard crust or the shepherd's pie. There is live Irish music from 9pm and the outdoor patio is perfect for warm summer evenings.

 The Market Lunch
MAP S5 ▪ Eastern Market, 225 7th St ▪ 202-547-8444 ▪ No credit cards ▪ Dis. access ▪ $

This lunchtime counter with nearby tables serves barbecue food North Carolina style, with a specialty in seafood. Try the crabcakes and oyster sandwiches. Saturday breakfast is very popular. No alcohol.

 Café Berlin
MAP S4 ▪ 322 Massachusetts Ave, NE ▪ 202-543-7656 ▪ Dis. access ▪ $

A German restaurant in a townhouse setting. *Wiener schnitzel*, pork loin with sauerkraut, and other hearty dishes are on the menu. The desserts are very tempting.

 Center Cafe Restaurant
MAP R5 ▪ 50 Massachusetts Ave, NE ▪ 202-898-0051 ▪ Dis. access ▪ $

Right underneath Union Station's dome, this eatery serves pizzas, paninis, sandwiches, and the like. It's a great place for people-watching.

 The Monocle
MAP S4 ▪ 107 D St, NE ▪ 202-546-4488 ▪ $$

The Monocle claims to be the first fine-dining restaurant on Capitol Hill. A favorite with the Kennedys, it's still popular with the power-dining crowd and is known for its well-hung steaks and ocean-fresh seafood.

 Johnny's Half Shell
MAP R4 ▪ 400 N Capitol St, NW ▪ 202-737-0400 ▪ Dis. access ▪ $$

An interesting seafood menu – try the kumamotos oysters, gumbo, or tequila-cured gravlax.

 Le Pain Quotidien
MAP S5 ▪ 660 Pennsylvania Ave, SE ▪ 202-459-9148 ▪ Dis. access ▪ $

A branch of the ubiquitous Belgian chain of light bite bakery cafés – the name means "daily bread."

 Bistro Bis
MAP R4 ▪ 15 E St, NW ▪ 202-661-2700 ▪ $$

A modern take on a French bistro with a stylish cherry-wood interior; deservedly popular.

 Tortilla Coast
MAP R5 ▪ 400 1st St, SE ▪ 202-546-6768 ▪ Dis. access ▪ $

Great Tex-Mex food. George W. Bush was a customer here before he was elected president.

 Sonoma
MAP S5 ▪ 223 Pennsylvania Ave, SE ▪ 202-544-8088 ▪ $$

California cuisine, cheese platters, and an eclectic menu of wines.

See map on pp78–9

The Mall and Federal Triangle

Even Washingtonians whose daily life rarely takes them to the Mall regard this magnificent grassy park as the heart of the city. It stretches 2.5 miles (4 km) from the Capitol to the east to the Potomac River, just beyond the Lincoln Memorial, to the west. Alongside and nearby are key symbols of the city and the nation: memorials to past suffering and triumphs, the workplaces of the federal government, and the Smithsonian museums. The Mall also serves as a national public square – it fills to capacity for the dazzling Fourth of July fireworks, and bustles daily with ordinary people jogging, strolling, or just enjoying the extraordinary views.

National Museum of American History

THE MALL AND FEDERAL TRIANGLE

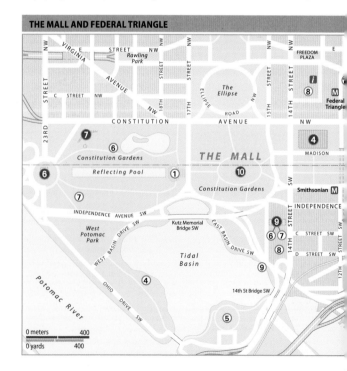

1 National Museum of the American Indian

MAP Q5 ■ 4th St, and Independence Ave, SW ■ Open 10am–5:30pm daily

This museum enshrines 10,000 years of Native American life and culture, and acknowledges the place of native peoples in the history of the Americas. The collection includes over 800,000 items, 7,000 of which are on display. Exhibits include pre-Columbian gold figurines, beadwork, textiles, and pottery from the Arctic to Patagonia. The building itself has been designed in harmony with Native American beliefs. The entrance faces east to meet the morning sun, and light spills in, reflecting the importance of the sun within Amerindian culture (see p54).

2 National Gallery of Art

Stroll through this building surrounded by illustrious artworks dating from before the Renaissance

The modern exterior of the National Museum of the American Indian

to the current day. The sculpture garden is a hit for its outdoor setting, summer jazz concerts, a winter ice-skating rink, and café (see pp24–7).

3 National Air and Space Museum

The story of flight, one of the most stirring in human history, is power-fully depicted in this favorite museum, renowned for its collection of precious artifacts of the challenging experience of flying (see pp20–21).

4 National Museum of American History

The story of the United States of America, from its beginnings to the present day, is told here through public icons and examinations of the daily lives of ordinary people. The many permanent exhibits include Julia Child's TV kitchen; the John Bull Locomotive; the Star-Spangled Banner Gallery; and "America on the Move," looking at modes of transport from 1876 to today (see pp22–3).

5 Hirshhorn Museum and Sculpture Garden

MAP Q5 ■ 7th St, at Independence Ave, SW ■ 202-633-4674 ■ Open 10am–5:30pm daily ■ Dis. access

The only public gallery in the city to focus solely on modern and up-and-coming art, this museum's holdings and exhibitions are exceptional. The unusual circular 1974 building provides a striking setting for outdoor sculpture in the surrounding plaza. Another sculpture garden across Jefferson Drive displays over 60 pieces of large-scale work (see p56).

Magnificent Lincoln Memorial and the Reflecting Pool

6 Lincoln Memorial

MAP M5 ▪ 23rd St, NW & Independence Ave ▪ Open 24 hours

This imposing marble memorial honors the US president who carried the country through its most difficult era. Designed by Henry Bacon (1866–1924) and featuring a monumental 19-ft (6-m) high statue of the seated Lincoln by Daniel Chester French (1850–1931), the memorial was dedicated in 1922. The Greek architecture reflects the ideals of its time *(see p50)*.

7 Vietnam Veterans Memorial

MAP M5 ▪ Constitution Ave & 21st St, NW ▪ Open 24 hours ▪ Dis. access

This stark remembrance features a black polished wall on which are inscribed the names of those who died during the Vietnam War. Controversial when it opened, because of its minimalism and because it failed to glorify the war, the memorial has become one of the most popular in the world. Its creator, the Chinese-American Maya Lin, was a 21-year-old student when she completed the design. More traditional statues were added in 1984 *(see pp50–51)*.

Vietnam Veterans Memorial

THE FEDERAL TRIANGLE

The area now known as the Federal Triangle was developed during Franklin D. Roosevelt's administration and improved by John F. Kennedy. Before then, the three-sided site, between 6th and 14th Streets and Pennsylvania and Constitution Avenues NW, was a run-down area. Its main buildings are the Federal Trade Commission, the National Archives, the Department of Justice, the Internal Revenue Service, and the R. Reagan Building and International Trade Center.

8 National Museum of Natural History

A favorite with children, yet filled with fascinating displays and artifacts that appeal to everyone, the vast halls of this Smithsonian museum have everything from the tiny bones of a snake to a giant ritual statue from Easter Island. Other exhibits include the vast Mammal Hall, Pacific Island canoes, fabulous gemstones (including the Hope Diamond), a giant squid, a set from a Chinese opera, and an Egyptian mummy case *(see pp28–9)*.

9 United States Holocaust Memorial Museum

MAP P5 ▪ 100 Raoul Wallenberg Place, SW (14th St between Independence Ave & C St) ▪ 202-488-0400 ▪ www.ushmm.org ▪ Open 10am–5:30pm daily; closed Yom Kippur, Dec 25 ▪ Dis. access

Among the city's most challenging sites, this museum is both a working study center for issues relating to the Holocaust and a national memorial for the millions murdered by the World War II Nazi government. The museum is solemn and respectful while engrossing and highly informative. Free timed passes are required to view the three-storey permanent exhibition. Passes can be obtained at the museum on the day of visit, or in advance online. There are some special exhibitions that can be seen without passes (see pp54–5).

10 Washington Monument
MAP P5 ■ 15th St between Independence & Constitution Aves ■ Open 9am–5pm daily (to 10pm in summer) ■ Dis. access ■ Entry by timed ticket

The plain Egyptian design of this radiant spire was largely the result of congressional cost-cutting, but now it seems an inspired choice. At 555 ft (165 m), the monument, built to honor the first president of the United States, towers over everything in the neighborhood and is ringed by 50 flags representing the 50 states of America. As a result of damage caused by a 5.8-magnitude earthquake in August 2011, the monument was closed for 32 months, reopening in May 2014. Visitors can now once more ascend by elevator to the 500-ft (152-m) high viewing deck for breathtaking views over the city.

Washington Monument

A MORNING WALK BY THE WATERFRONT

▶ Begin your walk at the **Franklin D. Roosevelt Memorial** (see p50) on West Basin Drive. There are hop-on-hop-off tour bus and trolley stops (see p124) directly in front (parking is limited). The sweep of this memorial carries visitors past waterscapes punctuated by engravings of the words of the president and evocative sculptures of his times.

On the left, leaving the memorial, is the little **Japanese pagoda** given to the city as a gesture of friendship by the mayor of Yokohama in 1958. Graceful Japanese cherry trees line the Tidal Basin bank beyond (see p72). Continue east across Inlet Bridge. About five minutes along the walkway stands the brilliant **Jefferson Memorial** (see p50), noted for its delicate design in spite of its size. Looking out from the steps here to the city is a wonderful experience.

Continue around the waterfront, cross Outlet Bridge, and bear to the left to the little boathouse, where you can rent a paddleboat for a unique view of the Tidal Basin (Open 10am–4pm daily; last boats out at 5pm • Adm). If you prefer to stay on dry land, continue north toward the **Washington Monument** and cross Maine Avenue leading to Raoul Wallenberg Place. On the right is the **US Holocaust Memorial Museum**. Before taking in the exhibits, gird yourself with some kosher fare in the **Museum Café** (see p91). Then spend the afternoon in remembrance of lives tragically lost under the Nazi regime.

See map on pp84–5 ←

The Best of the Rest

World War II Memorial

1 World War II Memorial
MAP N5 ▪ National Mall

This memorial includes 12 bas-relief sculptures depicting America at war *(see p51)*.

2 Enid A. Haupt Garden
MAP P5 ▪ 10th St & Independence Ave, NW ▪ Open Memorial Day–Sep: 6:30am–8pm daily; Oct–Memorial Day: 7am–5:45pm daily ▪ Dis. access

These formal gardens are designed to reflect the Smithsonian galleries above which they stand *(see p60)*.

3 National Archives of the United States
MAP Q4 ▪ 700 Pennsylvania Ave, NW ▪ 202-357-5000 ▪ Open 10am–5:30pm daily (to 7pm in summer) ▪ Dis. access

Home to foundation documents of the nation, including the Declaration of Independence.

4 Franklin D. Roosevelt Memorial
MAP N6 ▪ 900 Ohio Dr, SW

The inclusion of FDR's dog in the statuary indicates the human scale of this tribute *(see p50)*.

5 Jefferson Memorial
MAP N6 ▪ Tidal Basin

Words taken from the Declaration of Independence are engraved on the wall here *(see p50)*.

6 Constitution Gardens
MAP N5 ▪ National Mall

This 50-acre (200,000-sq-m) park's lovely centerpiece is an island in a tranquil lake, where markers honor the 56 signers of the US Constitution.

7 Korean War Veterans Memorial
MAP M5 ▪ 21st St & Independence Ave, SW

The 19 stainless-steel sculptures in this memorial to the 1953 Korean "police action" wrenchingly evoke the realities of war.

8 Bureau of Engraving and Printing
MAP P5 ▪ 14th St at C St, SW ▪ 202-874-2330 ▪ www.moneyfactory.org for tour info ▪ Open 8:30am–3:30pm Mon–Fri ▪ Dis. access

See millions of dollars being printed as you walk along the gallery.

9 National Museum of African Art
MAP Q5 ▪ 950 Independence Ave, SW ▪ Open 10am–5:30pm daily ▪ Dis. access

A program of changing exhibitions highlights a diverse collection of African pieces.

10 Old Post Office Pavilion
Closed for renovation

The Old Post Office Pavilion is undergoing major works to transform it into the Trump International Hotel, Washington, DC. Opening in 2016, the pavilion's old tower, with its fine views, will again open to the public.

Constitution Gardens

Items in Museum Stores

1 Smithsonian Teddy Bear
This is the Smithsonian's commemorative version of the Ideal Toy Company's 1902 bear, based on a famous *Washington Star* cartoon showing "Teddy" Roosevelt with a bear cub. In the National Museum of American History *(see pp22–3)*.

2 Jackie Kennedy Jewels
Who needs the real thing when reproductions of Jackie's most famous pieces can be purchased for next to nothing at the museum store at the National Museum of American History *(see pp22–3)*.

3 All Things Dinosaur
You will find lots of dinosaur merchandise for sale, including the Smithsonian book *Dinosaur!*, in the National Museum of Natural History *(see pp28–9)*.

4 Geodes and Fossils
The Gem and Mineral store has beautiful examples of geodes – sparkling crystals grown within hollows of other stones – and of fossils embedded in various matrixes. In the National Museum of Natural History *(see pp28–9)*.

5 Leather Flight Jackets
Good-quality leather jackets recreate the genuine flying jackets, and the selection and prices are reasonable. In the National Air and Space Museum *(see pp20–21)*.

6 Native American Art
Sculptures, carvings, ceramic pots, and plates created in intricate Native American designs can be purchased at the Museum of the American Indian *(see p85)*.

7 NASA Space Suits
Miniature orange suits, created with care and precise attention to detail, are available for little astronauts at the National Air and Space Museum *(see pp20–21)*.

Whistler's *Symphony in White, No. 1: The White Girl* in the National Gallery

8 National Gallery Prints
Many of the National Gallery's favorite paintings are available as quality prints, as well as in other forms ranging from phone cases to tote bags *(see pp24–7)*.

9 Chrysanthemum Satin Kimono
Gorgeous satin kimonos are among the magnificent fabric creations available at DC's two fine Asian museum stores. They also have unusual novelties such as *haiku* refrigerator magnets in the Arthur M. Sackler Gallery *(see p57)*.

10 Handmade Crafts
The Textile Museum's beautiful range of shawls and scarves, vibrant handbags, cute felt dolls, and inspiring textile-related books all make lovely gifts *(see p55)*.

See map on pp84–5

Children's Attractions

1 Johnson IMAX Theater
The movie screen at the Museum of Natural History is 66 ft high and 90 ft wide (20 m x 28 m), and some of the films shown are in 3-D and viewed using polarized glasses. Subjects include dinosaurs and the ocean (see pp28–9).

2 Smithsonian Carousel
■ MAP P5 ■ 1000 Jefferson Dr, SW ■ Open 10am–5:30pm daily weather permitting ■ Adm
This lovely carousel with its fancifully carved steeds is a treat for young and old alike. The sounds of the band organ are very cheering.

3 O. Orkin Insect Zoo
Live arthropods scamper and creep in this section of the Museum of Natural History – some can also be held (see pp28–9).

4 "How Things Fly"
Highly interactive exhibits and scheduled demonstrations at the National Air and Space Museum explain the principles that make flight possible. Kids can understand natural animal flight and human flight in contraptions from balloons to the space shuttle (see pp20–21).

5 Children's Film Program at the National Gallery of Art
Animations, environmental and nature films, and child's-eye views of life are compiled into lively shows the right length for children's attention spans (see pp24–7).

6 Daniel's Story, US Holocaust Museum
This exhibition, intended for children aged eight and older, is based on the actual experience of children during the Holocaust. It recounts the story of one German-Jewish boy's life between 1933 and 1945 (see pp86–7).

7 Einstein Planetarium
Astronomy is kid-friendly at the National Air and Space Museum in "One World One Sky: Big Bird's Adventure." The free, 20-minute show takes place on Fridays and the first consecutive Saturday and Sunday of the month. Book tickets in advance (see pp20–21).

8 Smithsonian Butterfly Garden
On the second floor of the National Museum of Natural History, this garden is a timed-entry exhibit. The four habitats – wetland, meadow, wood's edge, and urban garden – are all full of butterflies (see pp28–9).

9 Paddle the Tidal Basin
When the kids get tired of museums, head to the Tidal Basin to rent a paddle boat. A leisurely trip around the Basin will take you past FDR's tree-lined memorial and the stately Jefferson Memorial (see p88).

10 Ice Skating
The fountain in the National Gallery of Art Sculpture Garden (see p27) is frozen especially for ice skating in the winter, and visitors can rent skates on site.

Ice skating at the National Gallery of Art

See map on p84-5

Lunch Spots

PRICE CATEGORIES
For a three-course meal for one with half a bottle of wine (or equivalent meal), taxes and extra charges.

$ under $50 $$ $50–100 $$$ over $100

① Cascade Café & Gelato Bar
MAP Q4 ■ 3–7th St & Constitution Ave, NW ■ 202-712-7458 ■ Dis. access ■ $

Behind a glass wall in the National Gallery of Art concourse is a man-made waterfall. Facing this view is an attractive café with a wide range of hot and cold food.

② Paul Bakery and Café
MAP Q4 ■ 801 Pennsylvania Ave, NW ■ 202-524-4500 ■ $

An outlet of the famous French bakery, this café offers a wide variety of sandwiches, snacks, desserts, and organic breads.

③ Pavilion Café
MAP Q4 ■ 7th St and Constitution Ave, NW ■ 202-289-3360 ■ Dis. access ■ $

Sandwiches, salads, pizzas, and a variety of desserts are served in the Sculpture Garden at the National Gallery of Art.

④ Garden Café
MAP Q4 ■ 3–7th St and Constitution Ave, NW ■ 202-712-7458 ■ Dis. access ■ $

This little restaurant in the National Gallery of Art has the choice of a good buffet or a traditional à la carte menu. Surroundings of greenery combine with lofty ceilings.

⑤ The Source
MAP Q4 ■ 575 Pennsylvania Ave, NW ■ 202-637-6100 ■ $$

An Asian-influenced menu. The three-course, fixed-price lunch menu is recommended. Enjoy a casual dining atmosphere at this Newseum location.

Mitsitam Café

⑥ Mitsitam Café
MAP Q5 ■ National Museum of the American Indian, 4th St & Independence Ave, SW ■ 202-633-1000 ■ Dis. access ■ $

The name means "Let's eat" in Piscataway. The menu is inspired by Native American cuisine.

⑦ United States Holocaust Memorial Museum
The Museum Café serves traditional, kosher, and contemporary American favorites (see pp86–7).

⑧ Reagan International Trade Center Food Court
MAP Q4 ■ 1300 Pennsylvania Ave, NW ■ 202-312-1300 ■ Dis. access ■ $

This large food court has Texas grill, sushi, and dim sum as specialties. Photo ID is required for adults to enter the building.

⑨ Michel Richard Central
MAP P4 ■ 1001 Pennsylvania Ave, NW ■ 202-626-0015 ■ $$

Celebrity chef Michel Richard serves up French flavors and American concoctions such as lobster burgers and faux foie gras.

⑩ Atrium Café
The Museum of Natural History's café serves great grills, pizzas, and deli sandwiches using organic ingredients (see pp28–9).

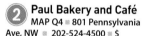

Following pages World War II Memorial

TOP 10 Penn Quarter

Lincoln's carriage at Ford's Theatre

Like other urban downtown areas, Washington's city center is filled with shops, hotels, restaurants, and theaters for every taste. Yet downtown Washington borders Pennsylvania Avenue – often called "America's main street." This is the direct route between the White House and the Capitol, and is therefore rich in historic associations. Presidential inauguration parades sweep down the avenue every four years; citizens protest here; President Lincoln was shot and died nearby. Washington's importance to world culture is reflected in the ease with which local restaurants and stores cater to an international clientele. The area draws visitors to the attractions of Chinatown, the Verizon Center, and the feeling of being at the center of the political world.

PENN QUARTER

1 Top 10 Sights
see pp95–6

1 Places to Eat
see p97

The Great Hall of the National Building Museum

1 Ford's Theatre
MAP Q4 ▪ 511 10th St, NW
▪ Open 9am–5pm daily ▪ 202-347-4833 ▪ Dis. access

John Wilkes Booth shot Abraham Lincoln in a balcony box here on April 14, 1865 – a tragic event that has made Ford's Theatre one of America's best-known historical sites. A museum contains Booth's .44 caliber Derringer pistol and other objects and information giving insights into Lincoln and the assassination plot. The restored building also houses theater productions. Directly across 10th Street is Petersen House, where Lincoln died after being carried from the theater (see p66).

Booth's Derringer pistol

2 National Building Museum
MAP Q4 ▪ 401 F St, NW ▪ Open 10am–4pm Mon–Sat, 11am–4pm Sun ▪ www.nbm.org ▪ Dis. access ▪ Adm; extra charge for special exhibits

This grand structure would be a fabulous place to visit even if it were empty. Its eight massive interior columns are among the largest in the world, and its immense interior space has beautiful natural light. The museum itself is dedicated to documenting and displaying important themes in the art and craft of building structures. It has permanent exhibitions on the city of Washington and on art created from tools, and mounts a stream of temporary exhi-bitions on topics such as the growth of urban transit and the development of architectural and construction methods. Other exhibits highlight the work of individual prominent architects. Families will particularly enjoy the Building Zone, where kids will be kept amused building towers and driving toy bulldozers.

3 Verizon Center
MAP Q4 ▪ 601 F St, NW ▪ Dis. access

While the Verizon Center is principally a sports arena, it has also become an unofficial community center. It draws crowds night after night with college and professional sports events, big-name concerts, circuses, figure-skating performances, and other events (see p67).

4 Newseum
MAP P4 ▪ 555 Pennsylvania Ave, NW ▪ Open 9am–5pm daily ▪ 202-292-6100 ▪ www.newseum.org ▪ Dis. access ▪ Adm

An awe-inspiring dissection of 500 years of the press. Visitors are able to compare media freedoms in 190 countries and view enlarged front pages from around the world that are updated daily. The 9/11 gallery and that of Pulitzer Prize photography are particularly moving. An unmiss-able museum experience (see p55).

5 National Museum of Women in the Arts

MAP P3 ■ 1250 New York Ave, NW
■ 202-783-5000 ■ Open 10am–5pm
Mon–Sat, noon–5pm Sun ■ Dis.
access ■ Adm

The collection of works by female artists here is among the world's best, ranging from Lavinia Fontana's *Portrait of a Noblewoman* (c.1580) to Frida Kahlo's 1937 *Self-Portrait Dedicated to Leon Trotsky (see p57)*.

6 US Navy Memorial

MAP Q4 ■ 701 Pennsylvania Ave, NW ■ Open 9:30am–5pm daily
■ Dis. access

The centerpiece of this delightful public space is a granite floor – a huge map of the world surrounded by fountains. A statue, dubbed "The Lone Sailor," overlooks the expanse *(see p51)*. A free film shows daily at noon.

7 International Spy Museum

MAP Q4 ■ 800 F St, NW
■ 202-393-7798 ■ Open
9am–7pm daily; closed
Thanksgiving, Dec 25
■ Dis. access ■ Adm

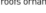

US Navy Memorial

More than just a great collection of spy gadgets from around the world, this museum encourages visitors of all ages to adopt a cover identity and learn how to react to real espionage challenges using interactive displays *(see p65)*.

8 Willard Hotel

MAP P4 ■ 1401 Pennsylvania Ave, NW
■ Dis. access

A glorious center of historic and political Washington. Every US president since 1853 has stayed as a guest or attended functions here. When Lincoln was inaugurated in March 1861, there were already assassination threats. Detective Alan Pinkerton

---

PENNSYLVANIA AVENUE

When the federal government moved to the city in 1800, Pennsylvania Avenue was selected as the "main street" because the area to the south was too muddy after rains, and the avenue offered a direct route from the President's House to the Capitol – at that time the only substantial buildings in town.

---

smuggled him into the Willard, and presidential business was conducted before the fireplace in the lobby.

9 National Portrait Gallery

MAP Q4 ■ 8th & F Sts, NW
■ Open 11:30am–7pm daily
■ Dis. access

The ornate 1836 building is a masterpiece in itself. The gallery celebrates remarkable Americans through visual and performing arts. Permanent exhibitions focus on individuals who have helped to shape the country's culture, from presidents and poets to villains and activists. The spectacular waved glass cover over the courtyard is by Norman Foster.

10 Chinatown

MAP Q3 ■ 7th & H Sts, NW

Now sadly diminished, but vestiges of Chinese culture can still be found among the upscale bars, restaurants, and shops. Look out for the Friendship Arch which marks the center, with seven pagoda-style roofs ornamented with 300 dragons.

Chinatown

Places to Eat

PRICE CATEGORIES

For a three-course meal for one with half a bottle of wine (or equivalent meal), taxes and extra charges.

....

$ under $50 $$ $50–100 $$$ over $100

1 Proof
MAP Q3 ▪ 775 G St, NW
▪ 202-737-7663 ▪ $$

Wine-lovers are drawn to this downtown hotspot known for its creative modern cuisine and a wine list of over 1,000 different varieties, including over 40 served by the glass.

2 Jaleo
MAP Q4 ▪ 480 7th St, NW
▪ 202-628-7949 ▪ Dis. access ▪ $

A fine *tapas* restaurant, Jaleo draws raves for its eggplant flan and sautéed shrimp. The atmosphere is lively, with great music and plenty of sangria.

3 Old Ebbitt Grill
MAP P4 ▪ 675 15th St, NW
▪ 202-347-4800 ▪ Dis. access ▪ $

Founded in 1856, this is the oldest saloon in the city, serving great hamburgers and seasonal entrées. Oyster bar in season.

4 Rosa Mexicano
MAP Q4 ▪ 575 7th St, NW
▪ 202-783-5522 ▪ Dis. access ▪ $$

"Mexican Pink" is a small national chain that serves upscale Mexican food, including an outstanding guacamole (made at the table in a traditional lava-rock mortar) and excellent cocktails.

5 Elephant and Castle
MAP P4 ▪ 1201 Pennsylvania Ave, NW ▪ 202-347-7707
▪ Dis. access ▪ $

Traditional British comfort food is served here in a homey pub-style atmosphere: the roast-beef-filled Yorkshire puddings, sausage and mash, and shepherd's pie are among the favorites.

Brasserie Beck

6 Brasserie Beck
MAP Q3 ▪ 1101 K St, NW
▪ 202-408-1717 ▪ $$

A paradise for beer-lovers, Beck offers several varieties and a large French–Belgian menu.

7 Full Kee
MAP Q3 ▪ 509 H St, NW ▪ 202-371-2233 ▪ $

This popular Chinatown Cantonese restaurant serves outstanding soups at an open station.

8 Oyamel
MAP Q4 ▪ 401 7th St, NW
▪ 202-628-1005 ▪ Dis. access ▪ $$

Traditional *antonjitos* and great cocktails at this Mexican eaterie.

9 Tony Cheng's Mongolian Restaurant
MAP Q4 ▪ 619 H St, NW ▪ 202-371-8669 ▪ $

The ground floor of this restaurant focuses on Mongolian-style barbecue while Cantonese cuisine and *dim sum* are served upstairs.

10 District Chophouse and Brewery
MAP Q4 ▪ 509 7th St, NW ▪ 202-347-3434 ▪ Dis. access ▪ $$

Hearty, meaty menus and on-site hand-crafted ales cater to sports fans from the Verizon Center.

See map on p94

🔟 The White House and Foggy Bottom

Bust of JFK, Kennedy Center

The majestic White House clearly defines this part of the city – many government buildings stand in the vicinity, including the old and new Executive Office Buildings, the Federal Reserve Building, and the State and Treasury Departments. To the west lies Foggy Bottom, a former swamp area now home to George Washington University. Farther west, the Kennedy Center stands on the Potomac waterfront. Throughout the area, as one would expect, restaurants, hotels, and stores provide the exceptional quality of service required by high-profile diplomats and politicians.

THE WHITE HOUSE AND FOGGY BOTTOM

1 Top 10 Sights
see pp99–101

① Places to Eat
see p103

1 The White House

Beautiful from any angle, the White House is a symbol of US political power and of democracy throughout the world *(see pp16–19)*.

2 Kennedy Center

MAP M4 ■ New Hampshire Ave at Rock Creek Parkway, NW ■ 202-467-4600 ■ Dis. access

A memorial to President John F. Kennedy, this huge performance complex – the largest in the country – presents the best expressions of the artistic culture he loved so well. National and international stars perform opera, concerts, musical comedy, drama, jazz, dance, and ballet. Located overlooking the Potomac, its terraces and rooftop restaurant offer spectacular views of the city below *(see p66)*.

3 Corcoran Gallery of Art

MAP N4 ■ 500 17th St, NW ■ 202-639-1700 ■ Call for opening times ■ www.corcoran.org ■ Dis. access

Designed by Ernest Flagg and completed in 1897, this building is one of the finest examples of Beaux Arts architecture in the United States. Note the atrium with its symmetrical gallery. Currently under rennovation it will reopen as a space for exhibiting pieces from traveling shows curated by the National Gallery of Art. It will also have iconic paintings from the original Corcoran collection housed in what will be called The Legacy Gallery.

4 Renwick Gallery

MAP N3 ■ 1661 Pennsylvania Ave, NW ■ 202-633-7970 ■ See http://americanart.si.edu for opening times

Having undergone extensive renovations, this Smithsonian museum is a gem, with its collections of fine American craft works and art. The second-floor Grand Salon served as a ballroom and site for special events when the Corcoran Gallery was located here before 1897. The 1859 structure, named after its architect, James Renwick, Jr., is a marvelous Second Empire-style building *(see p56)*.

5 Dwight D. Eisenhower Executive Office Building

MAP N4 ■ 17th St and Pennsylvania Ave, NW ■ 202-395-5895

This is another Second Empire building, but on a mammoth scale. Many people consider its highly embellished style and daunting pro-portions – with 300,000 sq ft (27,871 sq m) of office space on five storeys – to be magnificent, but others agree with esteemed author Mark Twain (1835–1910) and consider it to be "the ugliest building in America." The Departments of State, Navy, and War were housed here on its completion in 1888. Today, it houses the majority of offices for White House staff. Tours are suspended indefinitely.

GEORGE WASHINGTON UNIVERSITY

For the last 50 years, GWU has been a major presence in Foggy Bottom, contributing to its diversity and filling its streets with the energy of young students. Founded as Columbian College in 1821, the school adopted its current name in 1904 to honor the wishes expressed by George Washington **(below)** for the establishment of a major university in the city.

6 Treasury Building

MAP P4 ■ 1500 Pennsylvania Ave, NW ■ Tours currently only available for citizens and legal residents of the US, by appt only: 202-622-2000

The ornate Greek-Revival style of this building, designed in 1833, suggests a Temple of Money, and its imposing interior design confirms the seriousness with which the republic has always treated its currency. The restored Salmon P. Chase Suite and the Andrew Johnson Office reflect the gravity of official actions during and after the Civil War. The burglar-proof vault is always a hit with visitors, not least because of the beauty of its cast-iron walls and its demonstration of the lower security needs of a simpler time (see p49).

7 The Octagon Museum

MAP N4 ■ 1799 New York Ave ■ 202-626-7439 ■ Open 1–4pm Thu–Sat; Sun–Wed by appt ■ Dis. access

This unique and graceful building houses the oldest architecture museum in the country. It was designed by William Thornton, the original architect of the US Capitol Building, as a second home for John Tayloe III, a wealthy friend of George Washington. The house was completed in 1801 – one of the first private residences to be built to Pierre L'Enfant's plan – and provided shelter to President James Madison and his family while workers were rebuilding the White House after its destruction during the War of 1812. The exhibitions of the museum focus on the early Federal period of architecture, principally from 1800 to 1830.

8 Daughters of the American Revolution

MAP N4 ■ 1776 D St, NW ■ 202-628-1776 ■ Museum: Open 9:30am– 4pm Mon–Fri, 9am–5pm Sat; closed 2 weeks in July

The largest concert hall in the city is in Constitution Hall, the grand performance space operated by the Daughters of the American Revolution (DAR). The cornerstone of this John Russell Pope design was

Treasury Building

laid in 1928, using the same trowel George Washington used for the US Capitol building cornerstone in 1793. The DAR also contains a fascinating museum of early American artifacts, ranging from a simple 17th-century dwelling to an elaborate Victorian parlor. The DAR is also a volunteer women's service promoting patriotism, history, and education – any woman who can prove lineal descent from a patriot of the American Revolution is eligible to join.

9 Lafayette Park
MAP N3 ▪ H St between 15th and 17th Sts, NW

In DC's early years, this park served as a slave market, a racetrack, a zoo, and a graveyard. Today, it overlooks the North Portico of the White House, making it a favorite spot for TV news broadcasts, as well as a popular venue for protests and celebrations. The park and its surrounding buildings are a National Historic Landmark District. Of its five statues, the central one is of US President Andrew Jackson on his horse. The others, in the four corners of the park, are of foreign heroes of

Statue in Lafayette Park

the Revolution, including France's General Marquis Gilbert de Lafayette.

10 National Geographic Museum
MAP N3 ▪ 17th & M Sts, NW ▪ Open 9am–5pm Mon–Sat, 10am–5pm Sun ▪ Closed Dec 25 ▪ Dis. access ▪ Adm

The first-class exhibits here cover foreign cultures, nature, archeology, and *National Geographic's* signature breathtaking photography. Superb displays immerse visitors in their subject matter, all reflecting the diversity of our ever-changing planet.

A DAY EXPLORING 17TH STREET, NW

▶ MORNING

Begin your day with a tour of **Decatur House** *(see p48)*, a gorgeous Neo-Classical mansion. After the tour, turn left and walk to the end of the block; turn left onto 17th St, NW, and continue one block to Pennsylvania Ave. The **Renwick Gallery** *(see p99)* on the corner has a magnificent exterior and houses fascinating exhibits.

Continuing east on Pennsylvania, you can view the renowned north portico of the **White House** *(see pp16–19)* on your right. Reverse direction, return to 17th St, turn left to take in the ornate **Eisenhower Executive Office Building** *(see p99)*.

A block south is the **Corcoran Gallery of Art** *(see p99)*, with displays by the National Gallery of Art. Admire the Beaux Arts atrium here and grab a bite at the nearby Taylor Gourmet *(see p103)*.

AFTERNOON

After leaving the Corcoran, turn right and continue down 17th Street one block, to D Street. Turn right, and almost at the end of the block is the entrance of the **Daughters of the American Revolution**. In addition to the fascinating period rooms, the gift shop is a treat for anyone with an interest in quilting, samplers, or porcelain.

End your day by hailing a taxi on 17th Street to the **Kennedy Center** *(see p99)* and enjoy dinner at the **Roof Terrace Restaurant** *(see p103)*, with its breathtaking Potomac River views.

See map on pp98–9

Political Scandals

Benedict Arnold

1 Benedict Arnold

Arnold, in the early years of the Revolution, was a military leader on the Colonists' side. Yet, driven by money, he conspired to turn over to the British the army installation at West Point, of which he was then in command. When the plot was uncovered, he fled and then joined the British forces. His name became synonymous with "traitor."

2 Thomas Jefferson and Sally Hemings

The press commented in the early 1800s that Jefferson had had an affair and borne children with his slave, Sally Hemings. Jefferson denied the accusations, but DNA evidence makes the link probable.

3 Andrew Jackson and the Petticoat Affair

Margaret Eaton, wife of President Jackson's secretary of war, was rumored to have had a scandalous past. Jackson defended her honor and his enemies attacked, threatening his presidency.

4 "Boss" Shepherd

Alexander Shepherd pushed the Board of Public Works to great accomplishments in the 1870s, but he was later run out of town for bankrupting city government.

5 Whiskey Ring

In 1875, it was revealed that liquor taxes were being evaded by distillers and the officials they bribed. There were 110 convictions. President Grant secured the acquittal of his private secretary.

6 Teapot Dome

The oil fields at Teapot Dome, Wyoming, had been set aside as a reserve for the US Navy. In the 1920s, oil interests bribed government officials to lease the land to them, without competitive bidding.

7 Watergate

In 1972, President Nixon's re-election workers broke into the Democrats' Watergate offices to gather campaign information. When exposed by the *Washington Post*, the conspiracy, and President Nixon's involvement in the scandal, forced him to resign in 1974.

Watergate Committee members

8 Wilbur Mills and Fanne Foxe

Wilbur Mills, chairman of the powerful House Ways and Means Committee, was caught frolicking with his friend, stripper Fanne Foxe. He was forced to resign in 1974.

9 Iran-Contra Affair

In the 1980s, Ronald Reagan's administration carried out plans to secretly sell US weapons to Iran and use the proceeds to support Nicaraguan rebels. The investigation revealed deception and corruption.

10 Bill Clinton and Monica Lewinsky

Clinton's denial of sexual relations with the White House intern led to charges of perjury, obstruction of justice, and an investigation by the House of Representatives.

Places to Eat

PRICE CATEGORIES

For a three-course meal for one with half a bottle of wine (or equivalent meal), taxes and extra charges.

$ under $50 $$ $50–100 $$$ over $100

1 Blue Duck Tavern
MAP M3 ■ 1201 24th St, NW ■ 202-419-6755 ■ $$

The chef's specialties are prepared before your eyes in an open kitchen at this restaurant. Must-try dishes include thick fries cooked in duck fat, and mini apple pies.

2 Founding Farmers
MAP N3 ■ 1924 Pennsylvania Ave, NW ■ 202-822-8783 ■ Dis. access ■ $$

Both sustainable and stylish, this celebration of fresh food is brought to you by a collective of American family farmers.

3 Equinox
MAP N3 ■ 818 Connecticut Ave NW ■ 202-331-8118 ■ $$

A showplace for fresh local produce, Equinox chef Todd Grey is a pioneer in modern American cooking. The menu is seasonal and features many organic, sustainable ingredients.

Interior of Equinox

4 Georgia Brown's
MAP P3 ■ 950 15th St, NW ■ 202-393-4499 ■ Dis. access ■ $

Southern cooking with very generous portions of both food and attention. Chicken, fish, stews, corn bread, shrimp, and grits highlight the menu.

5 Marcel's
MAP M3 ■ 2401 Pennsylvania Ave, NW ■ 202-296-1166 ■ $$

Award-winning French and Flemish cuisine, including crispy skate wing and Carolina pheasant, wins rave reviews. There is a pre-theater menu available for $65.

6 Circle Bistro
MAP M3 ■ 1 Washington Circle ■ 202-872-1680 ■ Dis. access ■ $

Circle Bistro is close to Kennedy Center and is a great spot for pre-theater dinner and drinks.

7 Primi Piatti
MAP N3 ■ 2013 I St, NW ■ 202-223-3600 ■ $

A northern Italian restaurant with fine lamb dishes and other staples.

8 Roof Terrace Restaurant
MAP M4 ■ New Hampshire Ave at Rock Creek Parkway, NW ■ 202-416-8555 ■ Dis. access ■ $

At the Kennedy Center (see p99), this elegant restaurant has unrivaled views over the Potomac River.

9 Prime Rib
MAP N3 ■ 2020 K St, NW ■ 202-466-8811 ■ Closed Sun ■ Dis. access ■ $$

Steaks and chops dominate, also seafood and a vegetable platter. Jacket required for men.

10 Taylor Gourmet
MAP N4 ■ 1750 Pennsylvania Ave ■ Open 11am–7pm Mon–Fri & 11am–5pm Sat–Sun ■ $

Close to the White House, this hip version of a local deli chain makes the best sandwiches around.

See map on pp98–9

TOP 10 Georgetown

When Abigail Adams arrived in Washington in 1800, she described Georgetown as "the very dirtiest hole I ever saw." It was then a major port with a huge slave and tobacco trade, cheap housing, and commercial wharves. But the Chesapeake and Ohio Canal and the Baltimore and Ohio Railroad brought prosperity to Georgetown, and therefore style. When the canal began to fail, the district went with it, until Franklin D. Roosevelt partly rehabilitated the area. Its current modish status dates back to the Kennedy era, when Georgetown became fashionable.

Fountain in Dumbarton Oaks

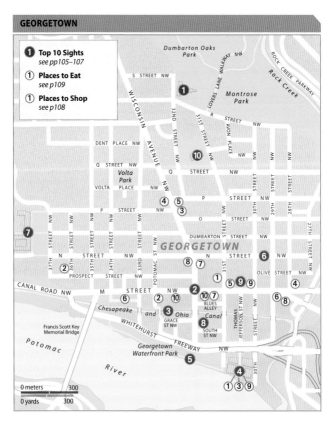

GEORGETOWN

1 **Top 10 Sights**
see pp105–107

1 **Places to Eat**
see p109

1 **Places to Shop**
see p108

1 Dumbarton Oaks Museum and Gardens

MAP L1 ■ 1703 32nd St, NW ■ 202-339-6401 ■ Museum open 2–5pm Tue–Sun; Gardens open Mar–Oct: 2–6pm Tue–Sun

This elegant Federal-style house, with its Philip Johnson-designed wing, houses a world-renowned collection of Byzantine and pre-Columbian artifacts. El Greco's *Visitation* is here also, possibly the Spanish master's last painting. The house and its museum are enclosed by acres of delightful landscaping, including a charming rose garden, a sparkling fountain terrace, and an orangery. In spring, this is one of the loveliest and most peaceful spots in the city to see cherry trees in blossom (see p49).

2 M Street and Wisconsin Avenue

MAP L2

This intersection is surrounded by the main shopping, entertainment, dining, and bar-crawling areas of Georgetown. The attractive shops surrounding Georgetown Park (see p69) include retailers of cool urban clothes, jewelry, fine wine, gourmet foods, art and antiques, and other specialties. Restaurant food of every description is available, from modern gourmet to street window kebabs.

3 Chesapeake and Ohio Canal

MAP L3 ■ Visitor Center: 1057 Thomas Jefferson St, NW ■ 202-653-5190 ■ Open 9am–4:30pm Wed–Sun; Closed winter

Like so many features of the area, the C&O Canal grew from a dream of George Washington's as a gateway to commerce with the west ("west" meaning Ohio at the time). Coal, flour, fur, timber, whiskey, iron ore, and other goods traveled on barges, towed by mules walking along canalside paths. The canal's commercial days are over, but its entire length from Georgetown to Maryland has been turned into one of the most beloved national parks.

Chesapeake and Ohio Canal

Visitors can experience the beauty and serenity of the canal by walking about a block south from M Street, NW, and turning west onto the towpath. The National Park Service Visitor Center for the C&O offers plenty of useful guidance for enjoying the canal. Guided tours and seasonal mule-powered barge rides are also available (see p60).

4 Washington Harbour

MAP L3 ■ 3000–20 K St, NW, at the bottom of Thomas Jefferson St, NW (between 30th & 31st Sts)

Dockside cafés and good restaurants; lovely views of the Potomac and the Kennedy Center; the Watergate complex and the Thompson boat-house; walkways for strolling, and benches for resting – all of these attractions and more make the harbor a magnet for Georgetowners. As a bonus, in winter the fountain area transforms into the largest outdoor skating rink in DC. The Washington Harbour residential and commercial building is an architectural exuberance designed by Arthur Cotton Moore and Associates.

Washington Harbour

5 Georgetown Waterfront Park

MAP L3 ▪ Water St, NW ▪ www.georgetownwaterfrontpark.org

This park runs along the Potomac between Washington Harbour and Key Bridge. A large, interactive fountain delights and dampens children on hot days and broad stone steps lead down to the water's edge.

6 N Street

MAP L2

Little attractions and oddities abound on this street, which is noted for its exemplary architecture. Best seen from the sidewalk on 28th Street, NW, the house at No. 2726 has an outstanding mosaic by Marc Chagall, a friend of the former owner. The elegant Federal house at No. 3038 was home to Ambassador Averell Harriman, who lent the house to Jacqueline Kennedy after her husband's assassination. She later bought the elaborate 1794 Thomas Beall House across the street. Lessons in 19th-century architecture can be learned from the Federal houses at Nos. 3327 and 3339, the Second-Empire home at No. 3025–7, and the Victorian homes of Wheatley Row at Nos. 3041–45.

A row of houses on N Street

7 Georgetown University

MAP K2 ▪ Gatehouse visitors booth: O & 37th Sts, NW ▪ Call for opening hours: 202-687-8299

This venerable institution sits on its hill overlooking Georgetown and the Potomac like a medieval citadel, its

Georgetown University

stone towers seemingly brooding with age. Yet the university is one of the most progressive in the country. Among the many interesting buildings here is the 1875 Healy Hall, built in an elaborate Flemish Renaissance style with surprising spiral adornment. Visitors can obtain campus maps and suggestions for strolls from the booth at the main gates.

8 Grace Church

MAP L3 ▪ 1041 Wisconsin Ave, NW (one block south of M St) ▪ Open by appt (tel: 202-333-7100) ▪ Office: Open 10am–6pm Mon, Tue, & Fri

The 1866 church construction was built to house a congregation founded to serve the boatmen and support staff of the C&O Canal. The simple

---

METRO CONNECTION AND BUS

Georgetown has no Metrorail station, and it used to be difficult for visitors to get to attractions here without a long walk from the nearest stations or a taxi ride. The Georgetown Metro Connection has been created to alleviate the problem. Running every 10 minutes daily, the shuttle bus provides inexpensive and convenient transportation to 13 locations from the Rosslyn and Dupont Circle metro stations. The Circulator Bus also runs every 5–10 minutes from 7am–9pm daily (see p118).

but extremely elegant design brings back the mid-19th century, although admittedly without the raucous bustle that must have accompanied the canal at its peak. The grounds are beautifully peaceful. The church offers poetry readings, theater performances, and concerts.

⑨ Old Stone House
MAP L2 ▪ 3051 M St ▪ 202-895-6070 ▪ Open noon–5pm daily ▪ Dis. access

This remarkable residence, dating from 1766, looks a little incongruous in the heart of the shopping area, but it provides a captivating window into 18th-century life. There are tours, and fascinating demonstrations of the crafts and tasks of colonial families.

⑩ Tudor Place
MAP L2 ▪ 1644 31st St, NW ▪ 202-965-0400 ▪ Tours of the House: 10am–4pm Tue–Sat, noon–4pm Sun; Gardens: open 10am–4pm Tue–Sat, noon–4pm Sun; closed Jan, federal holidays ▪ Dis. access ▪ Adm

This house-museum is remarkable for its beauty as well as its historic interest. Completed in 1816, it was built by Thomas Peter, son of a Georgetown tobacco merchant, and Martha Custis Peter, granddaughter of Martha Washington. The Peter family lived here for six generations and hosted many prominent guests.

Begin at **Washington Harbour** *(see p105)* for its views of the Potomac right on the waterfront. Take a pleasant stroll along the river before heading up **Thomas Jefferson Street, NW**, to the National Park Service Visitor Center for the **Chesapeake and Ohio Canal** *(see p105)*. In summer, you'll be able to take a mule-drawn barge ride.

Turn right and continue up Thomas Jefferson Street a short block and cross M Street, NW. In front of you is the **Old Stone House**. National Park Service interpreters recreate some of the daily activities that might have taken place in the house in the 18th century.

Reverse direction and return down Thomas Jefferson Street to the canal. Turn right onto the towpath and stroll for two blocks until you reach an opening in the embankment. Follow the steps to the right to **Wisconsin Avenue, NW**. Cross the street to lovely little **Grace Church**, built for the spiritual needs of workers on the canal. The grounds, with their mature trees, make a peaceful relaxation spot. Recross the canal and walk up Wisconsin to the shops at the **M Street, NW** intersection *(see p105)*.

Before an afternoon of retail therapy, turn left on M Street for lunch at **Clyde's of Georgetown** *(see p109)* or try one of the many sidestreet cafés.

Red door of Grace Church

Places to Shop

1 Old Print Gallery

MAP L2 ▪ 1220 31st St, NW

This gallery presents a huge collection of fine art prints arranged by themes. It is an outstanding source for political cartoons, city views, maps and charts, sporting and nautical prints, and historical subjects.

2 Dean & DeLuca

MAP L2 ▪ 3276 M St, NW
▪ Dis. access

The New York-originated gourmet food store is about as luxurious as a grocery store can get. The salad bar is superb, and the ready-made meals have brought success to countless Georgetown dinner parties.

3 Appalachian Spring

MAP L2 ▪ 1415 Wisconsin Ave, NW

This shop might as well be an informal museum, considering the quality of many of the handmade crafts for sale. The quilts, carved wood, pottery, and fabrics would grace any setting.

4 The Phoenix

MAP L2 ▪ 1514 Wisconsin Ave, NW

A charming, family-run store with contemporary clothing in natural fibers, classic jewelry, folk and fine art, unique items of homeware, and Mexican antiques.

5 Christ Child Society Opportunity Shop

MAP L2 ▪ 1427 Wisconsin Ave, NW

A treasure trove of antiques and collectibles, with proceeds going to charity. Best items upstairs.

6 Jeweler's Werk Galerie

MAP K3 ▪ 3319 Cadys Alley

A showplace of handcrafted jewelry and wearable art, tucked away in Georgetown's Cadys Alley design enclave. The store is stocked with intricate necklaces, earrings, and brooches by artists and designers.

John Fluevog Shoes

7 John Fluevog Shoes

MAP L2 ▪ 1265 Wisconsin Ave, NW

Canadian shoe designer John Fluevog brings his colorful, funky style and distinctive brand of comfortable, stylish/ugly (depending on your point of view) shoes to this historic quarter.

8 Bridge Street Books

MAP L3 ▪ 2814 Pennsylvania Ave, NW

Georgetown has few dedicated bookstores – this narrow, two-storey townhouse is fertile ground for anyone with a serious interest in literature, history, film, politics, philosophy, cultural studies or poetry.

9 Hu's Shoes

MAP L3 ▪ 3005 M St, NW

Visit this chic boutique for high-end women's shoes from emerging designers that you won't find in department stores.

10 Georgetown Tobacco

MAP L3 ▪ 3144 M St, NW

A neighborhood fixture for more than 40 years, this quaint tobacco shop sells more than 100 brands of cigars, hand-sculpted pipes, and humidors.

Places to Eat

1 Farmers Fishers Bakers
MAP L3 ▪ 3000 K St, NW
▪ 202-298-8783 ▪ $$

From the same folks that created
the phenomenally popular Founding
Farmers (see p103), this Washington
Harbour restaurant offers ultra-
fresh, agriculturally sustainable,
farm-to-table cuisine, with some-
thing for everyone – juicy steaks,
pizza, jambalaya, and ultra-fresh
sushi and fish dishes.

2 1789
MAP K2 ▪ 1226 36th St, NW
▪ 202-965-1789 ▪ $$

Serving excellent American food,
this elegant townhouse is divided
into five themed rooms, and was
popular with President Clinton
(see p68). Formal dress required.

3 Sequoia
MAP L3 ▪ 3000 K St, NW
▪ 202-944-4200 ▪ Dis. access ▪ $$

Famous for its beautiful views of
the Potomac River, this is a haven
for people-watching. The modern
American cuisine, emphasizing
seafood, enhances the setting.

4 Das Ethiopian Cuisine
MAP L2 ▪ 1201 28th St, NW
▪ 202-333-4710 ▪ $

The large Ethiopian population in the
city has produced a number of fine
restaurants; this one is rated among
the best. Delicious vegetarian dishes,
as well as spicy meat and poultry.

5 Miss Saigon
MAP L2 ▪ 3057 M St, NW
▪ 202-333-5545 ▪ Dis. access ▪ $

The vegetarian specials are popular
here, as well as the Vietnamese stir-
fries and curries.

6 Cafe Tu O Tu
MAP M2 ▪ 2816 Pennsylvania
Ave, NW ▪ 202-298-7777 ▪ $

This charming hole-in-the-wall
offers delicious Turkish-inspired
sandwiches, subs, and wraps.

7 Bistro Français
MAP L2 ▪ 3124 M St, NW
▪ 202-338-3830 ▪ $

Unpretentious French dishes and a
selection of wonderful pastries.

8 Martin's Tavern
MAP L2 ▪ 1264 Wisconsin Ave,
NW ▪ 202-333-7370 ▪ $

Good tavern fare, a great bar, and
a legendary booth in which John
F. Kennedy proposed to Jackie.

9 Fiola Mare
MAP L2 ▪ 3050 K St, NW
▪ 202-628-0065 ▪ Dis. access ▪ $$$

Impeccably prepared seafood, top-
notch service, and superb views
over the Potomac.

10 Clyde's of Georgetown
MAP L2 ▪ 3236 M St, NW
▪ 202-333-9180 ▪ Dis. access ▪ $$

This long-time Georgetown favorite
incorporates seasonal, local produce
into its special menu items.

Clyde's of Georgetown

See map on p104

🔟 Beyond the City Center

Mount Vernon greenhouse

Washington's monumental core is so rich in sights that visitors may be tempted to look no farther. But many delights lie within easy reach of the city center. The U Street NW corridor is an historic town center for the African-American community; Bethesda is full of fine restaurants; the Southwest waterfront is busy with commercial fishing activity; while Old Town Alexandria has a beautifully restored downtown. In complete contrast, there's the chance to experience the wilder side of the stately Potomac River at Great Falls.

BEYOND THE CITY CENTER

Silver Spring

Bethesda 🔟
② ③ ④

Rock Creek Park

⑨

13 miles (20 km)
➑

🔟 ③
① ⑥ ①

⑤

DISTRICT OF COLUMBIA

McLean

⑤
Tysons Corner

⑥ ⑥
⑨
Georgetown

WASHINGTON, DC

Arlington ②

Capitol Hill

Falls Church ⑤

⑦

ARLINGTON BOULEVARD

COLUMBIA PIKE

VIRGINIA

Anacostia

Ronald Reagan Washington National Airport

Annandale

SHIRLEY MEMORIAL HIGHWAY

Franconia

④ ⑦ ⑦ ⑨ 🔟
Alexandria ④

①

MARYLAND

Potomac River

① **Top 10 Sights**
see pp111–13

① **Places to Eat**
see p115

① **Shops**
see p114

Fort Hunt ②

➌

0 km   3
0 miles   3

Basilica of the National Shrine of the Immaculate Conception

1 Washington National Cathedral

This noble church, completed in 1990, is a triumph of the English Gothic style, hand-crafted using authentic methods (see pp30–31).

2 Arlington Cemetery

A visit to this solemn burial ground brings conflicting emotions – pride in the defenders of freedom, pleasure in the presence of its great beauty, but dismay at the loss of so many lives marked by the arrays of headstones (see pp34–5).

3 Mount Vernon

Without a doubt the finest current view of George Washington the man, and of the agrarian plantation life that was an important stream leading to the revolutionary break with Britain (see pp36–9).

4 Old Town Alexandria
MAP D5

This lovely old city center, across the Potomac just beneath the capital, retains the charm and hospitality of its illustrious past while giving visitors all modern conveniences, including a metro station (King Street on the yellow and blue lines). Alexandria is noted for its historical and archeological museums, Gadsby's Tavern (see p113), the evocative system of Civil War forts and defenses at Fort Ward, and its captivating residential architecture, civilized shops, and restaurants.

5 Basilica of the National Shrine of the Immaculate Conception
MAP D3 ▪ 400 Michigan Ave, NE ▪ 202-526-8300 ▪ Open Nov–Mar: 7am–6pm daily; Apr–Oct: 7am–7pm daily ▪ Dis. access

This mammoth basilica, dedicated in 1959, incorporates more than 60 chapels and oratories that retell the diverse history of the Roman Catholic Church in the United States. Conceived in the grand style – it is the largest Roman Catholic church in the Western hemisphere – the building combines Byzantine and Romanesque features, creating an intensely decorative but substantial effect. The interior is overwhelming in its grandeur, whatever your faith. There is also a cafeteria serving breakfast and lunch on the site, which is convenient because there are few nearby restaurants. Free docent-guided tours are available.

Old Town Alexandria

6 U Street, NW
MAP N1

For much of the 20th century, U Street, NW, was the main street of this bustling and prosperous African-American neighborhood. Opened as a movie theater in 1922, the Lincoln Theatre *(see p67)* has now been refurbished and presents performances of every kind. Next door is the famous Ben's Chili Bowl, turning out great simple food for capacity crowds. The legendary jazz musician Duke Ellington *(see p47)* played his first paid performance at True Reformer Hall at the junction of 12th and U Street, NW. The poignant sculpture and plaza of the African-American Civil War Memorial *(see p51)* commemorates African-Americans who served their country in the Civil War.

Ben's Chili Bowl shop sign

7 Southwest Waterfront
MAP D4 ▪ Water St, SW

This is a wonderful place for strolling, summer and winter. The diversity of Washington is on parade, the sail-boats, yachts, and houseboats are picturesque, and the seafood – both cooked and raw – at the Southwest Fish Wharf is a showcase of what's best in eastern waters. The Fish Wharf is the current lively, raucous embodiment of colorful markets that have flourished here continuously since about 1790. It is famed for its crabs, oysters, and clams, and also specializes in river fish not widely available elsewhere, such as perch and bass.

8 National Air and Space Museum Steven F. Udvar-Hazy Center
14390 Air and Space Museum Pkwy, Chantilly, VA 20151

This display and restoration center for some of the museum's magnificent collection of historic aviation and space artifacts *(see pp20–21)* opened in December 2003 near Dulles International Airport at the intersection of routes 28 and 50. Two giant hangars with accompanying support buildings provide over 760,000 sq ft (70,611 sq m) of much-needed extra display space.

National Air and Space Museum Steven F. Udvar-Hazy Center

9 Great Falls
MAP A2 ■ Great Falls Tavern
Visitor Center: 11710 MacArthur Blvd
■ 310-767-3714 ■ Open dawn–dusk
daily

About 15 miles (24 km) north of
Washington, DC, the Potomac is
rent by magnificent waterfalls over
the crags and sluices of the eroded
river bed. In the state of Virginia,
Great Falls Park is reached from
Old Dominion Drive (Route 738).
It provides spectacular overlooks
above the river, hiking trails, and the
ruins of a small 19th-century town.
On the Maryland side, the Great Falls
area is part of the C&O Canal (see
p105). The Great Falls Tavern Visitor
Center offers canal rides, hiking, and
ranger-led tours, and there are
remarkable river views from the
overlook on Olmstead Island.

Whitewater rapids at Great Falls

10 Bethesda, Maryland
MAP C2

Locally, Bethesda is best known for
its enormous quantity and range of
restaurants, most of them clustered
into a lively downtown area that still
retains the charming atmosphere of
a traditional town center. The high-
end professional employment offered
by Bethesda's world-renowned bio-
technology industry, however, has
also generated a spirited music,
performance, and arts scene that
caters to its cultured and wealthy
residents. The city is especially
strong on public art. Its streets
and parks spotlight distinguished
contemporary works in every style,
by way of sculpture and stunning
painted murals.

A DAY IN OLD TOWN ALEXANDRIA

▶ **MORNING**

Begin at **Christ Church** (118 N
Washington St; Open 9am–4pm
Mon–Sat, 2–4pm Sun; Donation),
a handsome Georgian-style
building completed in 1773.
George Washington's box pew
has been preserved. Then turn
right onto Cameron Street toward
the harbor. Continue three blocks
and turn right onto North Royal
Street. The two buildings on your
right comprise **Gadsby's Tavern
Museum** (see p48). The tours are
a fascinating introduction to
colonial life in the city.

Continue one block and turn left
onto King Street. On Saturday
morning, it hosts an historic
Farmers Market. Continue south
to the **Stabler-Leadbeater
Apothecary Museum** (107 S
Fairfax St; Open 11am–4pm Wed–
Sat, 1pm–4pm Sun; Adm). Here
you will find herbal botanicals,
handblown glass, and medical
equipment from the 1800s.

AFTERNOON

Enjoy lunch or a snack at one of
the many restaurants along King
Street, then continue toward the
harbor to North Union Street, and
turn left to the **Torpedo Factory**
(see p114). Directly behind it, the
Potomac Riverboat Company
(potomacriverboatco.com) runs
cruises of Alexandria Seaport.

Shop for original artwork at
the popular **Torpedo Factory Art
Center**, home to more than 80
working artist studios open to
the public, plus six galleries and
the Bread & Chocolate Café,
which serves light fare.

Shops

1 National Harbor
MAP D6 ▪ 165 Waterfront Street, National Harbor, MD 20745

Sixty shops line the streets of this trendy neighborhood. Designer jewelry and fashion are prominent, as are specialty shops selling fine foods, wines, and even motorcycles. Nearby Tanger offers another 85 brand-name outlets.

2 Mount Vernon Antique Center
MAP C6 ▪ 8101 Richmond Hwy, Alexandria, VA 22309

This is one of the oldest and best-known antiques malls in the area, with over 30 independent dealers selling a vast array of items. The very popular Modern Montage offers mid-20th-century furniture and kitsch.

3 Politics and Prose
MAP H2 ▪ 5015 Connecticut Ave, NW

A bookstore with a large selection of works on politics, culture, and government. A cheerful place, despite its serious stock, with a coffee bar.

4 Fibre Space
MAP C5 ▪ 1219 King Street, Alexandria, VA 22314

This Old Town Alexandria shop is filled with a dazzling assortment of colorful yarns from local, sustainable sources. Knitting equipment can be found here as well: needles, crochet hooks, patterns, and more.

5 Tysons Corner Center and Galleria At Tysons II

Buses run from Ballston Metro to this huge shopping site, with stores catering to every budget as well as cinemas and restaurants (see p69).

6 Kramerbooks
MAP N2 ▪ 1517 Connecticut Ave, NW

This Dupont Circle landmark has a fantastic collection of books and knowledgeable staff. There's also

Afterwords Café at Kramerbooks

a bar and restaurant, the Afterwords Café. The store is open 24 hours on Fridays and Saturdays.

7 Torpedo Factory Art Center
MAP D5 ▪ 105 N Union St, Alexandria

The building was originally a factory to manufacture torpedoes. Today, the site contains 82 studios and six galleries where artists and crafts-people create work and offer it for sale on site. Prints, ceramics, photography, painting, and sculpture.

8 Sullivan's Toy Store
MAP G4 ▪ 4200 Wisconsin Ave, NW

An astounding range of playthings can be found in this store, but the real stars are the items with a link to the past: model kits, craft supplies, board games, and kites.

9 Copenhaver
MAP N2 ▪ 1301 Connecticut Ave, NW

Appreciating the formalities of communication, Copenhaver sells the tools for it: elegant writing paper, envelopes, pens, and inks.

10 Kron Chocolatier
MAP G2 ▪ Mazza Galleria, 5300 Wisconsin Ave, NW

This store is famous for its molded chocolate items – bears, sports cars, even the US Capitol. They also sell greeting cards made of chocolate.

Places to Eat

PRICE CATEGORIES

For a three-course meal for one with half a bottle of wine (or equivalent meal), taxes and extra charges.

$ under $50 $$ $50–100 $$$ over $100

1 Two Amys
MAP H4 ■ 3715 Macomb St, NW ■ 202-885-5700 ■ Dis. access ■ $

Within easy walking distance of the National Cathedral, this is Washington locals' favorite pizzeria – expect to wait for a table during peak times. Authentic Neapolitan pizzas baked in a wood-burning oven.

2 American Tap Room
MAP C2 ■ 7278 Woodmont Ave, Bethesda, MD ■ 301-656-1366 ■ Dis. access ■ $

This modern version of the traditional American tap room offers an inviting atmosphere, a large selection of beers, and a classic grill menu. Open for brunch, lunch, and dinner.

3 Bacchus of Lebanon
MAP C2 ■ 7945 Norfolk Ave, Bethesda, MD ■ 301-657-1722 ■ Dis. access ■ $

The *mezze* at this Lebanese restaurant are delicious. Marinated chicken, roast eggplant (aubergine), hummus, and squid fill numerous little dishes with flavor.

4 Passage to India
MAP C2 ■ 4931 Cordell Ave, Bethesda, MD ■ 301-656-3373 ■ $

The Indian menu here does not limit itself to any particular region of India. The *daal* and butter chicken are rich and smooth.

5 Grand Cru
MAP C4 ■ 4401 Wilson Blvd, Arlington, VA ■ 703-243-7900 ■ $$

This tiny café has an exquisite menu, including succulent *filet mignon* and moreish *crème brûlée*. Doubling as a wine shop, its choice is outstanding. Dine in the courtyard in good weather.

6 Ardeo+Bardeo
MAP H4 ■ 3311 Connecticut Ave, NW ■ 202-244-6750 ■ $$

This is a hip bistro/bar delivering new American cuisine. Book a roof deck table in summer.

7 Bilbo Baggins Restaurant
MAP D5 ■ 208 Queen St, Alexandria, VA ■ 703-683-0300 ■ Dis. access ■ $

The menu fuses dishes from around the world and features a wonderful selection of beers.

8 Jackie's Restaurant
MAP D2 ■ 8081 Georgia Ave, Silver Spring, MD ■ 301-565-9700 ■ $$

Housed in a redesigned auto parts garage, Jackie's adds a touch of fun to eating out. Enjoy a modern American menu including free-range meats, organic produce, and seafood.

Interior of Restaurant Eve

9 Restaurant Eve
MAP D5 ■ 110 S. Pitt St, Alexandria ■ 703-706-0450 ■ $$

Wood and amber create a cozy ambience here. There is a cocktails and nibbles lounge, a bistro, as well as a tasting room. Don't miss the butter-poached Maine lobster.

10 Taverna Cretekou
MAP D5 ■ 818 King St, Alexandria, VA ■ 703-548-8688 ■ $

Fantastic Greek food, ouzo, and traditional dancing can be found at this popular restaurant.

See map on p110

Streetsmart

**U Street African-American Civil War
Memorial / Cardozo metrorail station**

Getting To and Around Washington, DC

Arriving by Air

Three major airports serve Washington, DC, with most international flights arriving at **Dulles International** (IAD) 26 miles (42 km) west of the city. **Baltimore-Washington International** (BWI) is 30 miles (48 km) northeast of DC. **Reagan National Airport** (DCA) is just 5 miles (8 km) from the city center.

Transportation from each of the airports into the city center can be accessed direct from the baggage claim area.

From Dulles airport the **Washington Flyer Silver Line Express Bus** goes to the Wiehle-Reston East Memorial station for transit on the Metrorail. **SuperShuttle** shared vans provide a service throughout the area, or take a cab or **Uber**.

From BWI, there is train service on the **Maryland Rail Commuter Service** (MARC) and **Amtrak**. There is an express **Metrobus** service to Greenbelt Metrorail Station. **SuperShuttle** and taxi service is also available.

Reagan National offers **Metrorail**, **SuperShuttle**, **Washington Flyer Express Bus** and taxi service.

Arriving by Train

Amtrak provides intercity rail transport, stopping at Union Station in Washington, DC. For travel between DC and Boston, **Acela Express** is the quickest way to reach New York and other major East Coast cities. Amtrak has a reduced-fare USA Rail Pass, which is worth considering if traveling widely across the country.

Arriving by Car

Washington streets are congested most of the time, and often gridlocked during rush hours (6:30am–9:30am and 4–7pm). There is limited parking available near the attractions, making driving a less attractive option than public transportation. Some of the larger hotels have parking, and public lots are available. Driving routes to DC are I-95 and I-270 from the north, I-66 from the west, I-95 and I-395 from the south, and US 50 from the east. I-95 and I-495 form a heavily used interstate beltway around Washington, DC.

Arriving by Bus

The main bus terminals are behind Union Station, with some lines stopping across the street. **Greyhound Lines** connect with over 3,700 locations, and offer budget passes. Other lines include **Bolt Bus**, **Megabus**, and **dc2nyc**.

Traveling by Metrorail

For most destinations in the city, **Metrorail**, the subway-surface rail system, is the best way to get around. Service is frequent, cars are clean and comfortable, stops are convenient to major sights, and the system is among the safest in the world. Fares depend on the time of day and distance traveled, from $1.95 to $5.75. There are 1-day, 7-day, and 28-day passes that allow unlimited trips for a reduced fare. Metro stations are marked with a large "M," and system maps and fares are posted on the mezzanine level where the station manager is available to answer questions. Available at Metro stations, SmarTrip fare cards offer lower fares and use on Metrorail, **Metrobus**, **Circulator**, and other regional transit systems.

Traveling by Metrobus and the Circulator

The public bus system serves all areas of the city. Exact change is required (regular routes are $1.80). Circulator buses travel five useful routes every 10 minutes. Exact change is required ($1.00 fare). It is worth buying a SmarTrip card at a Metrorail station for convenience and discounts on Metrorail, Metrobus and Circulator, and for free bus-to-bus transfers.

Traveling by Car

Driving is undoubtedly the least efficient way to get around in the core DC area. There are few gas stations, one-way streets, and time-of-day parking restrictions. The streets are laid out in a grid, with numbered streets running north–south, while the east–west streets are named with letters. Diagonal streets named after states crisscross the grid in both directions. Addresses contain NE, SE, SW, or NW indicating position relative to the Capitol building, which is at the center of the grid.

Parking in a lot will cost you about $20 per day or about $12 for two hours. Street parking meters have a two-hour maximum stay, and fines are high. Parking is prohibited on a great many downtown streets during rush hour, with hours posted on curbside signs. Your car will be towed if you disregard them.

Zipcar is an hourly car rental program. Plan members (pre-approved plus $50 membership) can reserve a car for pick up at a Metro station. Rates start at $7.75 (gas and insurance included). **Car2Go** rents tiny Smart cars by the minute. The subscription service **Uber** lets you summon a ride-share car or a taxi by smartphone, billing your credit card.

Rental car companies are located at airports, Union Station, and many other locations. You can find one with Yellow Pages (www.yellowpages.com). Renting a car requires a valid driver's license and a major credit card, and drivers must be at least 25 years old.

Traveling by Taxi

Taxis in DC are metered, and there are more than 100 companies from which to choose. You'll find them waiting outside most hotels. Expect to pay a "drop" fee of $3.25, and 27 cents every one-eighth of a mile. Bulky luggage and additional passengers will be charged as extra. The maximum base fare within the district is $19.00.

Walking and Biking in Washington

Washington is a city built for walking, with wide sidewalks and courteous drivers. Busy streets have pedestrian walk lights at intersections. But the central attractions of the city are quite spread out, so pack a pair of comfortable shoes. **Bikeshare** has bicycles for hire at around 300 locations. One day, three day or monthly passes are available.

DIRECTORY

AIRPORTS

Baltimore/Washington International (BWI)
800-435-9294
bwiairport.com

Dulles International Airport (IAD)
703-572-2700
mwaa.com

Reagan National Airport (DCA)
703-417-8000
mwaa.com

AIRPORT TRANSFERS

Maryland Rail Commuter Service (MARC)
410-539-5000
mtamaryland.com

SuperShuttle
800-258-3826
supershuttle.com

Washington Flyer
washfly.com

TRAIN

Amtrak
800-USA-RAIL/800-872-7245
amtrak.com

BUS LINES

Bolt Bus
boltbus.com

dc2nyc
dc2nyc.com

Greyhound
greyhound.com

Megabus
megabus.com

PUBLIC TRANSPORTATION

Circulator
292-567-3040
dccirculator.com

Metrorail and Metrobus
202-637-7000
wmata.com

TAXIS

GoCurb taxi app
www.gocurb.com

Yellow Cab Company of DC
202-546-7900
dcyellowcab.com

CAR/BIKE RENTAL

Avis
avis.com

Budget
budgetrentacar.com

Capital Bikeshare
capitalbikeshare.com

Car2Go
car2go.com

Hertz
hertz.com

Uber
www.uber.com

Zipcar
zipcar.com

Practical Information

Passports and Visas

Canadian and Mexican visitors require valid passports to enter the US. Citizens of 38 countries, including most European nations, Australia and New Zealand, do not need a visa, but must apply to enter in advance via the **Electronic System for Travel Authorization (ESTA)** and have a valid passport. All other visitors require a tourist visa and passport to enter, and will be photographed and have their fingerprints checked. A return airline ticket is required. Entry regulations may change, so check well in advance of travel with the **US Department of State** for the latest regulations.

Customs and Immigration Regulations

Nonresident travelers need to complete a **Customs and Border Protection Agency** form. Passengers may carry $100 in gifts; one liter of alcohol as beer, wine or liquor (age 21 years or older); and one carton of cigarettes, 50 cigars (not Cuban) or two kilograms (4.4 lbs) smoking tobacco without incurring tax.

Travel Safety Advice

Visitors can get up to date travel safety information from the **Foreign and Commonwealth Office** in the UK, the **US Department of State** and the **Department of Foreign Affairs and Trade** in Australia.

Travel Insurance

Emergency medical insurance is highly recommended for international travelers to the US, as costs for medical and dental care can be very high. Travel insurance against trip cancellation, air travel delays, and lost baggage is also advisable. Car rental agencies offer vehicle and liability insurance, but check your policy before traveling.

Health

No vaccinations are required for visiting the United States. For ease of moving through airport security, pack any items of essential medication in their original labeled containers. Unused syringes are allowed along with injectable prescription medication such as insulin.

Hotels will often be able to recommend a doctor if you require medical assistance. Or contact a service such as **In-House Doctor** whose members will come to your room. Walk-in clinics are also available, and for minor injuries some pharmacies have nurse practitioners available for walk-in care.

The **CVS** drugstore chain has 24-hour pharmacies at Dupont Circle; 2240 M St, NW; 1199 Vermont Aww, NW; and 4555 Wisconsin Ave, NW. These can refer you to pharmacies in other areas. **Georgetown Hospital** provides a free physician referral service 9am–5pm Monday to Friday. The **District of Columbia Dental Society** operates a free phone referral service from 8am–4pm daily. For immediate treatment in an emergency, call 911 for an ambulance.

Personal Security

Washington is a large, cosmopolitan city and is generally safe in the tourist areas. Petty crime does exist, so be alert to your surroundings, leave your valuables and passport in a hotel safe, avoid wearing flashy jewelry and the excessive display of expensive cameras or smartphones. Keep your wallet in an inside pocket, or carry a purse across your chest for safety. Bring back-up copies of valuable and important documents and identification, and keep them in your room safe. Split your cash and credit cards between wallets and pockets. Keep your hotel room locked, and get a receipt for stored luggage. Do not leave your luggage or other belongings unattended.

The eastern part of DC is a rapidly gentrifying area and is generally safe, but there are areas of the city where extra vigilance and care are required, especially at night. Ask your hotel concierge for advice if you are unsure.

The likelihood of your recovering stolen property is slim, but it is essential that you file a claim with the **Metropolitan Police Department (MPDC)** and retain a copy of the crime report for your insurance company at home. Note the taxi company, bus line or metro route you use to help retrieve belongings accidentally left behind. If you lose your passport or believe it to have been stolen, you will need to get in touch with your embassy immediately. Call your credit card company or bank to report lost or stolen cards or travelers' checks.

Law enforcement in DC is provided by multiple national agencies, which include blue-uniformed **MPDC** officers who patrol the city streets and are able to assist visitors. Park Rangers wear gray shirts and green trousers and help visitors on park property. There are also Secret Service and Special Weapons and Tactics teams, whose job is to maintain national security and protect the president.

Currency and Banking

The US currency is the dollar, and the dollar is made up of one hundred cents. The most commonly used dollar bills come in denominations of $1, $5, $10, and $20. Cents are available in one (penny), five (nickel), ten (dime), and 25 (quarter) cent coins.

It is best to convert a small amount of currency at the airport to cover immediate expenses, and then convert larger amounts at a bank from the teller or the ATM machine, using a debit card. Cirrus, Plus and NCYE are the more common networks. For safety, use an ATM inside a bank. Bank ATM machines also accept credit cards, but interest will be charged. Currency bureaus such as **Travelex** and the **International Currency Exchange** are to be found at airports, Union Station, and in other key locations.

A major credit card is required for car rentals, and most hotels, restaurants, and services accept Visa, Mastercard, and American Express. Cash is often required by street vendors, on buses, and for some services.

DIRECTORY

CUSTOMS AND VISAS

Customs and Border Protection
Visa Waiver Program, Customs information
ⓦ cbp.gov/travel

Electronic DC Embassy List
ⓦ embassy.org

Electronic System for Travel Authorization (ESTA)
ⓦ esta.cbp.dhs.gov/esta

Transportation Security Administration
ⓦ tsa.gov/traveler-information

TRAVEL SAFETY ADVICE

Australia
Department of Foreign Affairs and Trade
ⓦ dfat.gov.au
ⓦ smartraveller.gov.au

UK
Foreign and Commonwealth Office
ⓦ gov.uk/foreign-travel-advice

US
US Department of State
ⓦ travel.state.gov

EMERGENCY

Medical, Ambulance, Police, Fire (all emergencies)
☏ 911

Metro transit police
☏ 202-962-2121

MPDC Police non-emergency
☏ 311 or 202-737-4404

PHARMACIES

CVS (24-hour pharmacies)
MAP N2 ▪ 6 Dupont Circle
☏ 202-785-1466
MAP G3 ▪ 4555 Wisconsin Avenue NW
☏ 202-537-1587

WALK-IN CLINICS AND IN-HOUSE SERVICES

CVS (minor injuries)
MAP G3 ▪ 4555 Wisconsin Avenue NW
☏ 202-537-1587

Farragut Medical & Travel Care
MAP N3 ▪ 815 Connecticut Ave NW
☏ 202-775-8500

In-House Doctor
☏ 202-216-9100

HOSPITALS

Children's Hospital National Medical Center
☏ 202-476-5000

DC Dental Society
☏ 202-547-7613

Emergency Dental
☏ 888-661-2852
(24-hours a day)
ⓦ emergency.dentistphone.com

Medical Referral Services
☏ 202-342-2400

Medstar Georgetown University Hospital
☏ 202-444-2000

CURRENCY

International Currency Exchange
Dulles International and Regan National airports
ⓦ iceplc.com

Travelex
MAP S4 ▪ Union Station
☏ 202-371-9220
ⓦ travelex.com
MAP N3 ▪ 1800 K St. NW
☏ 202- 872-1428

Communications

All telephone numbers in the United States are ten digits long. The first three of these are the area code, which is 202 for Washington, DC, 703 for nearby Virginia and 240, 301 or 410 for Maryland. Dial the area code first, followed by the seven-digit phone number. Dial 0 for operator, and 411 for directory assistance (fee). To make a direct overseas call, dial 011, the country code, city area code, and number. For an operator-assisted call, dial 01, country code, city area code, and number.

Public telephones can be found in airports and train stations, but not in many other places. It is most convenient to use a cell phone as hotels add a substantial service fee to calls made from your room. Before traveling, check with your phone carrier about service in the United States. You can rent a phone from **Cellhire**, **Cellular Abroad** and others for overseas and US calls, or buy a disposable phone at convenience stores, office supply stores, or phone outlet stores for use within the US.

Most hotels offer free Wi-Fi, but some hotels charge for this service. Free Wi-Fi is available at many coffee shops and libraries, and at several of the Smithsonian Museums as well as the National Gallery of Art on the National Mall. Free Wi-Fi locations are shown on the **dc.gov** website.

Many hotels sell stamps and will mail your letters. A standard (one ounce) letter costs $.49 to a US destination, or $1.15 outside the US. Flat rate envelopes and boxes are available at post offices (Mon–Fri, 9am–5pm) for both domestic and overseas destinations.

The internationally respected *Washington Post* newspaper covers local news, politics and entertainment; national and international news. Its pull-out *Friday Weekend* section and *Going Out Guide* cover Washington entertainment and events. *USA Today*, the *Wall Street Journal* and the *New York Times* newspapers are also widely available. The monthly *Washingtonian Magazine* has a good local events calendar.

The major television networks include CBS (channel 9), NBC (channel 4), FOX (channel 5), and ABC (channel 7). Many others are available though cable TV, which is provided by many hotels. Radio station WTOP (1500 AM) is an all-news and weather station, and WAMU (88.5 FM) is a member of National Public Radio.

Opening Hours

Business office hours are usually 9am–5pm. Stores open at 9am or 10am and close around 5pm or 6pm Mon–Sat. Some stores remain open later, and Sunday store hours vary. Most banks are usually open 9am–5pm Mon–Fri, and some open Sat am. Grocery stores generally open 8am–9pm daily, or longer. Some larger stores are open 24 hrs. Pharmacy hours vary, from 8am–6pm and later, and some have 24-hour service. Most museums are open 10am–5:30pm, but check each listing individually, as opening times and dates can vary. Metrorail hours begin at 5am Mon–Fri and 7am Sat–Sun, and close at midnight Sun–Thu and 3am Fri–Sat. Schedules over public holidays may be different, so check ahead of time.

Time Difference

Washington, DC is on Eastern Standard Time (EST), and is 3 hours ahead of California and 5 hours behind London. Daylight Savings Time starts on the second Sunday in March and ends on the first Sunday in November with the change officially taking place at 2am.

Electrical Appliances

The standard US electric current is 110 volts, and 60 Hz current. American plugs have two flat pins; an adapter will be needed for European appliances.

Driving License

Foreign visitors with a valid license from most countries are permitted to drive personal or rental cars while in the United States, but it is advised to carry an International Driving Permit (IDP) if you plan on renting a car or driving, especially if the license is not in English, does not have a photo, or is not from a qualifying country. An IDP must be obtained in the country that originally issued the driver's license.

Sources of Information

Washington, DC Chamber of Commerce provides information for visitors on their website and by mail. The site has search capabilities for hotels, shops, restaurants, tourist sights, and transportation.

Destination DC provides information on the city's history, attractions, dining, accommodation, tours, and events, and offers useful interactive maps. Assistance is available by phone and in person at their office on 7th St.

Weather

Average daytime temperatures in DC range from a high of 89°F (32°C) in July to a low of 42°F (6°C) in January, and average nighttime temperatures from a high of 72°F (22°C) in July to a low of 26°F (-3°C) in January. However, temperatures in every season vary greatly. Humidity can be an issue in summer, so always carry some water with you when out and about. Precipitation averages range from a high of 4in (10cm) in August to a low of 3in (7cm) in January when much of it falls as snow. Winters can be very windy and raw, with snow and ice storms that can paralyze the city.

Disabled Visitors

Washington, DC is one of the most accessible cities in the US, but there are challenges involved with some historic buildings, restaurants, and shops. MetroRail stations and trains are accessible, featuring extra-wide fare gates and elevators. Rail cars have gap reducers, priority seating, and emergency intercoms. All Metrobuses are wheel-chair accessible with the ability to "keel" or lower, and have lifts or ramps. Disabled visitors can apply for a **Metro Disability** ID card and discounted fares. Allow at least three weeks for application approval. The Metro website offers videos and downloadable guides. Government buildings, museums and theaters are accessible, but verify that tours can meet your requirements. It is advisable to call hotels and restaurants ahead of time and ask about the specific amenities available.

Shopping Tips

Shopping is a popular activity in Washington, but it is unusual to find bargains in the district unless it is sales season. A six percent sales tax is added to the purchase price. No-sales-tax weeks take place two or three weeks before Christmas, and shave extra off prices that are often already reduced. Black Friday, the day after Thanksgiving, offers big discounts, and post-Christmas sales are also a magnet for shoppers. Promotions are common on other public holidays as well.

Unique souvenirs can be found at museum shops and gift stores at other major attractions, in the form of high-quality items related to their collections, history, or special features.

Trips and Tours

Bus tours are one of the most popular sightseeing options, and several bus tour companies feature double-decker vehicles with open-topped upper decks that allow for unlimited viewing. The **Old Town Trolley** runs National Mall/Downtown, National Cathedral and Arlington Cemetery loops. Passengers can hop on and off at any stop, and one- or two- day passes are available. Similar services are also offered by **Big Bus Tours** and **City Sights**.

The city's abundance of sidewalks and green spaces make walking tours one of the best ways to see specific areas like the Mall, Capitol Hill, and Georgetown. Guided or self-guided walking tours generally last between one and three hours and can cover a lot of ground, so dress for changeable weather, carry drinking water, and wear comfortable walking shoes.

Bicycle tours are also popular and offer the advantage that they can cover long distances more quickly than is possibly on foot. A rather different way to tour the city is on a two-wheeled electric **Segway**. Potomac River cruises range from luxury lunch and dinner tours as you watch the sights of the city glide past, to thrilling land-and-water trips aboard an amphibious **DC Ducks** craft.

There is also a wide array of special interest tours covering topics such as food, history, art, or espionage, or you could design your own itinerary.

Dining Tips

Washington, DC has more than 1,000 restaurants serving almost every cuisine imaginable, and prices range from affordable to very expensive. Many more are available nearby in Virginia and Maryland. A 10 percent tax is added to the dining total, and a tip of 15–20 percent of the bill is expected. Wine, beer, and alcoholic beverages are readily available in many restaurants. The strictly enforced legal age for drinking alcohol is 21, and photo ID may be requested from patrons of any age.

Many restaurants are casual, reasonably priced, and serve families. Breakfast is generally served from 7–10am, lunch from 11:30am–2pm and dinner from 5:30–10pm. Food is generally available all day in central DC, especially at the Smithsonian Museums, Capitol Visitor Center, and the food courts at Union Station and the Ronald Reagan Building.

The Washington Post provides a comprehensive online dining guide, and reservations at many DC restaurants can be made through **OpenTable**, which has reliable reviews.

Local specialties include fresh seafood from Chesapeake Bay, and from May–September steamed crack-your-own Chesapeake Blue Crabs are served at **The Quarterdeck**, a casual eatery on the waterfront in Arlington. Maryland crab cakes and she-crab soup are regional favorites, and can be tried in many restaurants.

Locals, dignitaries, and in-the-know visitors head to **Ben's Chili Bowl** for a half-smoke, which is a mildly spicy chili and cheese covered smoked sausage hot dog. Bring the kids, and enjoy the atmosphere, great food, and reasonable prices.

Farm-to-table dining features fresh, seasonal local or regionally grown foods. **Founding Farmers** provides a friendly upscale setting with community tables. The new American menu offers roast chicken, pot pie, green salads, sandwiches, and more.

For a great take-out, head to a deli. **Dean & Deluca** in Georgetown offers a wide variety of fresh-made local, regional, and international dishes, gourmet foods, and a great choice of fine wines.

Where to Stay

Washington offers a wide range of accommodation options, and hundreds of properties to choose from. High-rise hotels, historic inns, all-suites accommodations, and trendy boutique hotels can be found near the main attractions and Metro stations. Bed and breakfasts, apartments, and campgrounds are usually located farther from the city center.

Prices are lowest from January through early March, although popular mid-February Valentines Day rates are higher. Spring and summer are popular and generally expensive, although weekend rates may be lower when Congress is not in session. Book well in advance.

Check with booking sites such as **Visit DC**, **Destination DC**, and **Hotels.com** for discount rates; **Kayak** and **Expedia** for discounted airline and hotel packages; and hotel websites for special promotions and package deals. All rates are subject to an additional 14.5 percent room tax, and it is customary to tip porters at least $1 for each bag carried, and housekeeping $1–2 a day.

When selecting a hotel, look for included amenities that will make your stay more comfortable. Some rooms are more spacious than others, and some provide small refrigerators, micro-waves, or free Wi-Fi. Suite accommodations may have a sofa bed in a living area in addition to the bedroom, and often have a full kitchen. Swimming pools, exercise facilities, and breakfasts are sometimes included.

Bed-and-breakfast inns are available outside the central area, and can be booked through agencies such as **Bed and Breakfast DC**. Some include full breakfast, accept children, and offer free Wi-Fi.

Furnished apartments are available, and often provide more space and amenities at a lower price than hotels. They usually have a full kitchen but no maid service and are often located in residential neighborhoods. **Vacation Rentals** and **Vacation Rentals by Owner** both offer many properties.

Another useful option is the international agency **Airbnb**, which lists furnished apartments as well as less expensive shared-space bedrooms within a range of personal residences. Washington has only one hostel, **Hostelling International**.

There are two camp-grounds located in Maryland that provide transportation service for visitors to DC, **Cherry Hill Park** and **Capitol KOA**.

DIRECTORY

TRIPS AND TOURS

Bicycle Tours
Ⓦ bikethesites.com

Boat Tours
Ⓦ capitolriver cruises.com
Ⓦ potomacriver boatco.com
Ⓦ dcducks.com

Bus Tours
Ⓦ oldtowntrolley.com
Ⓦ bigbustours.com
Ⓦ citysights.com

Segway Tours
Ⓦ bikethesites.com
Ⓦ capitalsegway.com
Ⓦ citysegwaytours.com

Custom Tours
Ⓦ washingtondctour guides.com

Food Tours
Ⓦ dcmetrofood tours.com

Walking Tours
Ⓦ spiesofwashington tour.com
Ⓦ dcbyfoot.com
Ⓦ washington walks.com

DINING

Ben's Chili Bowl
MAP P1 ▪ 1213 U Street NW, Washington DC 20009
Ⓒ 202-667-0909
Ⓦ benschilibowl.com

Dean & Deluca
MAP L3 ▪ 3276 M Street NW, Washington DC 20007
Ⓒ 202-342-2500
Ⓦ deandeluca.com

Founding Farmers
MAP N3 ▪ 1924 Pennsylvania Ave NW, Washington, DC 20006
Ⓒ 202-822-8783
Ⓦ wearefounding farmers.com

Open Table
Ⓦ opentable.com

Quarterdeck
MAP K5 ▪ 1200 Fort Myer Drive, Arlington, VA 22209
Ⓒ 703-528-2722
Ⓦ quarterdeckarlington.com

Washington Post
Ⓦ washingtonpost.com/ goingoutguide/ restaurants/

ACCOMMODATION

Airbnb
Ⓦ airbnb.com

Bed and Breakfast DC
Ⓦ bedandbreakfast dc.com

Capitol KOA
Ⓦ koa.com

Cherry Hill Park
Ⓦ cherryhillpark.com

Destination DC
Ⓦ washington.org

Expedia
Ⓦ expedia.com

hotels.com
Ⓦ hotels.com

Hostelling International
Ⓦ hiwashingtondc.org

Kayak
Ⓦ kayak.com

Vacation Rentals
Ⓦ vacationrentals.com

Vacation Rentals by Owner
Ⓦ vrbo.com

Visit DC
Ⓦ visitdc.com

Places to Stay

PRICE CATEGORIES
For a standard, double room per night (with breakfast if included), taxes and extra charges.

$ under $200 $$ $200–350 $$$ over $350

Historic Hotels

Tabard Inn
MAP 2 F2 ■ 1739 N St, NW ■ 785-6173
■ tabardinn.com ■ $
This boutique hotel, named for the inn in Chaucer's *The Canterbury Tales*, is converted from three townhouses. The rooms are charming and eclectic; some are Victorian. Several of the rooms have a shared bath. The restaurant serves superb American-Continental cuisine and there's a wood-paneled lounge-bar with live jazz.

Woodley Park Guesthouse
MAP J5 ■ 2647 Woodley Road, NW ■ 202-667-0218 ■ dcinns.com ■ $
This 15-room guesthouse occupies a Victorian house and is a great bargain in an expensive city. You may have to share a bath in the hall, but the Victorian-style rooms are immaculate and the location near the National Zoo can't be beat.

Churchill Hotel
MAP M1 ■ 1914 Connecticut Ave, NW ■ 202-797-2000
■ thechurchillhotel.com ■ Dis. access ■ $$
Opened as the Highlands apartment building in 1906, this Beaux Arts grand hotel provides huge rooms with panoramic views over the Potomac.

Henley Park Hotel
MAP Q3 ■ 926 Massachusetts Ave, NW ■ 202-638-5200
■ henleypark.com
■ Dis. access ■ $$
The outside of this Tudor-manor-style hotel is festooned with gargoyles, and the interior boasts original stained glass and antique furniture.

The Jefferson
MAP N2 ■ 16th & M Sts, NW ■ 202-448-2300
■ jeffersondc.com
■ Dis. access ■ $$-$$$
The Jefferson's Beaux Arts facade is particularly eye-catching. Public areas feature displays of historic prints, documents, and paintings, including some associated with Thomas Jefferson. This elegant hotel is a popular choice with celebrities.

Renaissance Mayflower Hotel
MAP N3 ■ 1127 Connecticut Ave, NW ■ 202-347-3000
■ renaissancemayflower.com ■ Dis. access ■ $$
Opened in 1925 to a huge crowd on the day of Calvin Coolidge's presidential inauguration, this hotel has hosted every Inaugural Ball since. Harry S. Truman stayed here during White House renovations; Franklin D. Roosevelt wrote his 1933 inaugural address here; and J. Edgar Hoover had lunch here most days.

Hay-Adams Hotel
MAP N3 ■ 16th and H Sts, NW ■ 202-638-6600
■ hayadams.com ■ Dis. access ■ $$$
Constructed on the sites of the homes of John Hay and Henry Adams, across Lafayette Square from the White House, this elegant hotel features beautifully restored rooms furnished with antiques and ornamental ceilings, and with stunning views.

Morrison-Clark Inn
MAP P3 ■ 1015 L St, NW ■ 202-898-1200 ■ morrisonclark.com ■ $$$
Created from two townhouses, this mansion served as the Soldiers, Sailors, Marines, and Airmen's Club for 50 years. Decorative touches remain, including four gorgeous mirrors.

Phoenix Park Hotel
MAP R4 ■ 520 N Capitol St, NW ■ 202-638-6900
■ phoenixparkhotel.com
■ Dis. access ■ $$$
Named after the iconic Dublin park, this hotel, in a stately 1920s Georgian Revival building, has an Irish theme, right down to the live music and house ales at the in-house pub.

St. Regis Hotel
MAP N2 ■ 923 16th St, NW ■ 202-638-2626
■ stregis.com/washington
■ Dis. access ■ $$$
If both Queen Elizabeth II and the Rolling Stones chose to stay here, the St. Regis must be doing something right. Calvin Coolidge took part in the 1926 opening of this grand hotel, styled after

a Renaissance palace and appointed with antiques, chandeliers, and fine tapestries.

W Washington, DC

MAP P4 ■ 514 15th St, NW ■ 202-661-2400 ■ whotels.com/washingtondc ■ Dis. access ■ $$$

The historic Hotel Washington is now Hotel W, a prestigious property of Starwood Hotels and Hotels. Located next to the White House, many of its rooms have superb views of this and other major landmarks. It offers exceptional service in a luxurious setting.

Willard Inter-Continental

MAP P4 ■ 1401 Pennsylvania Ave, NW ■ 202-628-9100 ■ willardintercontinental.com ■ Dis. access ■ $$$

This is undoubtedly among the most historic of the city's hotels. World events, including the birth of the League of Nations, were discussed here by leading figures, and royalty from all over the world have been its guests.

Luxury Hotels

Gaylord National Resort and Convention Center

MAP D6 ■ 201 Waterfront St, National Harbor, MD ■ 301-965-2000 ■ gaylordhotels.com ■ $$

Located south of the city, the Gaylord National is the largest combined hotel and convention center on the East Coast. The 18-storey glass atrium offers great views of the Potomac River and Alexandria.

Grand Hyatt Washington

MAP P3 ■ 1000 H St, NW ■ 202-582-1234 ■ grand hyattwashington.com ■ Dis. access ■ $$

The location is superb and the airy atrium includes a lagoon with an island on which a pianist plays. The sports bar is a popular meeting place.

Hyatt Regency Washington on Capitol Hill

MAP R4 ■ 400 New Jersey Ave at D St, NW ■ 202-737-1234 ■ hyattregency washington.com ■ Dis. access ■ $$

This bustling hotel takes up an entire block. It is within easy walking distance of the Capitol and the Smithsonian.

Loews Madison Hotel

MAP P3 ■ 1177 15th St, NW ■ 202-862-1600 ■ madisonhoteldc.com ■ Dis. access ■ $$-$$$

Located close to the White House, this chic hotel provides comfortable guestrooms, some with covered terraces. Free Wi-Fi throughout.

The Fairfax

MAP M2 ■ 2100 Massachusetts Ave, NW ■ 202-293-2100 ■ luxurycollection.com ■ Dis. access ■ $$$

The Georgian-style decor here is complemented by modernity in the form of large LCD TVs, iPod docks, and DVD players. Located at a prime Embassy Row location, the hotel attracts diplomats, and celebrities looking for discretion. A concierge and a fitness room are available 24 hours a day.

Fairmont Washington DC

MAP M2 ■ 2401 M St, NW ■ 202-429-2400 ■ fairmont.com ■ Dis. access ■ $$$

This hotel's garden courtyard is gorgeous, and there's a great pool and gym area, plus business facilities. Some rooms have delightful balconies.

Four Seasons Hotel

MAP L3 ■ 2800 Pennsylvania Ave, NW ■ 202-342-0444 ■ fourseasons.com/washington ■ Dis. access ■ $$$

This is one of DC's best five-star hotels. The spa is renowned, and afternoon tea at the Garden Terrace will make any visitor feel special. It's convenient to Georgetown and Rock Creek Park.

The Graham Hotel

MAP 2 D3 ■ 1075 Thomas Jefferson St NW, 20007 ■ 202-337-0900 ■ thegrahamgeorgetown.com ■ $$$

The Graham offers every luxury in the heart of Georgetown, with spacious, tranquil suites and a roof-deck bar.

Mandarin Oriental Washington, DC

MAP P5 ■ 1330 Maryland Ave, SW ■ 202-554-8588 ■ mandarinoriental.com ■ Dis. access ■ $$$

Monumental views over the Potomac Tidal Basin and Jefferson Memorial are plentiful at this elegant hotel. Rooms boast king beds and silk tapestries, as well as luxurious amenities such as plasma TVs and Wi-Fi. There is also a fitness center, pool, and spa.

Park Hyatt Washington

MAP M2 ■ 24th St at M St, NW ■ 202-789-1234 ■ parkwashingtonhyatt. com ■ Dis. access ■ $$$
The decor at this hotel features original moden artwork enhancing its elegant ambience. The hotel has an skylit indoor pool and a fitness center.

The Ritz-Carlton

MAP M3 ■ 1150 22nd St, NW ■ 202-835-0500 ■ ritzcarlton.com ■ Dis. access ■ $$$
The Ritz-Carlton provides the finest quality furnishings – including Egyptian cotton sheets and down pillows – to make guests comfortable. The marble bathrooms are luxurious. Also, traditional pool and fitness and spa facilities.

Boutique Hotels

Hotel Lombardy

MAP N3 ■ 22019 Pennsylvania Ave, NW ■ 02-828-2600 ■ hotel lombardy.com ■ $
This hotel is decorated with imported fabrics, Oriental rugs, and original art. It is now pet-friendly too. The restaurant is bistro-style.

George Washington University Inn

MAP M3 ■ 824 New Hampshire Ave, NW ■ 202-337-6620 ■ gwuinn. com ■ Dis. access ■ $$
The handsome, large guest rooms and suites of this inn are colonial-inspired, but each come equipped with a refrigerator, microwave, and coffee-maker. Some even have complete kitchens. The Kennedy Center and Metro are nearby.

Hotel Madera

MAP N2 ■ 1310 New Hampshire Ave, NW ■ 202-296-7600 ■ hotelmadera.com ■ $$
Offering modern comfort with a vibrant, stylish twist, this small hotel exudes elegance and sophistication.

Hotel Monaco

MAP Q4 ■ 700 F St, NW ■ 202-628-7177 ■ monaco-dc.com ■ Dis. access ■ $$
Housed in the 19th-century General Post Office building. Hotel Monaco's stately façade conceals a colorful, modern interior and an award-winning on-site restaurant, Poste.

Hotel Palomar

MAP M2 ■ 2121 P St, NW ■ 202-448-1800 ■ hotel palomar-dc.com ■ $$
This funky boutique hotel offers luxury accommodation in a lively neighborhood. Larger rooms have spa-style bathrooms, and there's an outdoor pool and sundeck.

Melrose Hotel

MAP M3 ■ 2430 Pennsylvania Ave, NW ■ 202-955-6400 ■ melrosehoteldc.com ■ Dis. access ■ $$
A modern hotel in the heart of town, the Melrose is known for its refined luxury. The furnishings are contemporary but with classic influences.

Sofitel Lafayette Square

MAP P3 ■ 806 15th St, NW ■ 202-730-8800 ■ sofitelwashingtondc. com ■ Dis. access ■ $$
On a corner of Lafayette Square, this 1862 building has been transformed by the French Sofitel chain into an elegant hotel with a gentleman's club-like ambience. The sound-proofing and acoustic doors are a welcome feature. The restaurant serves contemporary French bistro cuisine.

Topaz Hotel

MAP N2 ■ 733 N St, NW ■ 202-393-3000 ■ topazhotel.com ■ $$
The striking interiors here are in the highest contemporary style along with exquisite design. The Topaz Bar is among the best in the city. Some rooms include yoga and fitness equipment.

Capella Washington

MAP M3 ■ 1050 31st St, NW ■ 202-617-2400 ■ capellahotels.com ■ Dis. access ■ $$$
Billed as an "urban luxury retreat," the Capella Washington is located on Georgetown's riverfront. This top-notch boutique hotel offers spa services, a fitness center, a rooftop pool and lounge area, plus a full service restaurant and bar.

The Hotel George

MAP R4 ■ 15 E St, NW ■ 202-347-4200 ■ hotel george.com ■ Dis. access ■ $$$
One of the most fashionable hotels in the city, deserving the attention because of its innovative design, excellent business facilities (the desks are huge slices of granite with contemporary communications), and its fine bistro-style restaurant. The in-room CD player/radio provides sound environments including ocean, brook, and forest.

Business Hotels

Courtyard Washington Convention Center

MAP Q4 ■ 900 F St NW ■ 202-638-4600 ■ courtyard.com/wascn ■ Dis. access ■ $
Situated in a former 1891 bank but completely up to date, and with an indoor pool and fitness center. The hotel has two conference rooms.

Crystal City Marriott

MAP D4 ■ 1999 Jefferson Davis Highway, Arlington VA ■ 703-413-5500 ■ marriott.com ■ $
This hotel has excellent business amenities and is convenient for the Pentagon and close to Reagan National Airport. There are 13 meeting rooms and a walkway to a shopping mall.

Embassy Suites

MAP M2 ■ 1250 22nd St, NW ■ 202-857-3388 ■ washingtondc.embassysuites.com ■ Dis. access ■ $
Part of the Hilton Group, this hotel offers well-furnished rooms with good work areas and a separate living room. Conference rooms with extensive equipment are available for rent. There's also an indoor swimming pool and fitness center.

Hamilton Crowne Plaza Hotel

MAP P3 ■ 14th and K St, NW ■ 202-682-0111 ■ hamiltondchotel.com ■ $
This is a distinguished hotel, where the guest rooms offer a desk with high-speed internet and voicemail, and cable TV with in-room movies. Pets are welcome.

Omni Shoreham Hotel

MAP J5 ■ 2500 Calvert St, NW (near Connecticut Ave) ■ 202-234-0700 ■ omnihotels.com ■ Dis. access ■ $
Adjacent to Rock Creek Park, this grand hotel sits in acres of landscaped grounds. A luxury hotel, it has hosted countless important guests. The business center includes clerical support and there are large meeting rooms.

One Washington Circle Hotel

MAP M3 ■ 1 Washington Circle, NW ■ 202-872-1680 ■ thecirclehotel.com ■ $
Business travelers receive excellent service at this Foggy Bottom hotel. A knowledgable staff manages the five meeting rooms, and suites have lots of seating space for work. Larger suites have full kitchens and walk-out balconies. There is also an outdoor pool.

Washington Court Hotel

MAP 4 E3 ■ 525 New Jersey Ave NW, 20001 ■ 628-2100 ■ washingtoncourthotel.com ■ $$
Rooms are sleek and modern with free Wi-Fi and flatscreen TVs, and some have stunning views of the Capitol.

Capital Hilton

MAP N3 ■ 1001 16th St at K St, NW ■ 202-393-1000 ■ hilton.com ■ Dis. access ■ $$$
This hotel is in a great location, just two blocks from the White House, and offers all the usual Hilton facilities, plus a health club and spa.

Marriott Wardman Park

MAP J5 ■ 266 Woodley Rd, NW ■ 202-382-2000 ■ marriott.com ■ Dis. Access ■ $$$
Close to Rock Park Creek and surrounded by cute little stores and restaurants, this is the largest convention hotel in Washington. It combines charm with modern services and technology. There are scores of meeting rooms and an exhibition area. The well-maintained rooms offer all business services.

Washington Hilton

MAP N1 ■ 1919 Connecticut Ave, NW ■ 202-483-3000 ■ washington.hilton.com ■ Dis. access ■ $$$
The garden setting is lovely, and the elevated location gives a fine view of the city skyline. Both the layout and size of this complex, including its rooftop pool and sun deck, make for a resort-like atmosphere, while staff and facilities offer every amenity.

The Westin Georgetown

MAP 2 E2 ■ 2350 M St NW, 20037 ■ 429-0100 ■ westingeorgetown.com ■ $$$
Marble bathrooms with extra-deep bathtubs are among the amenities in the rooms of this well-appointed hotel. There is an outdoor pool and a leafy courtyard garden, with a choice of the Caucus Room French brasserie or the Latin-American Bóveda tavern for in-house dining. Pets are permitted by prior reservation.

For a key to hotel price categories see p126

The Westin Penn Quarter

MAP 3 B2 ■ 1400 M St NW, 20005 ■ 429-1700 ■ westinwashington dccitycenter.com ■ $$$
A large hotel with great weekend special deals, two full-service restaurants, plus an on-site Starbucks. Four blocks from the McPherson Metro, the Westin has a large central atrium and all the amenities one would expect for a largely business clientele. The hotel also provides a 24-hour fitness center, and is pet-friendly.

Family-Friendly Hotels

The Avenue Suites

MAP M3 ■ 2500 Pennsylvania Ave, NW ■ 202-333-8060 ■ avenuesuites.com ■ Dis. access ■ $
This excellent Georgetown location provides a 24-hour gym, generous living rooms, large TVs, iPod docking, high-speed internet, and a fully equipped kitchen including a dishwasher. Pets are allowed.

Fairfield Inn and Suites

MAP Q3 ■ 500 H St, NW ■ 202-289-5959 ■ marriott.com ■ Dis. access ■ $
Formerly the Red Roof Inn, this hotel has been revamped by Marriott and is now geared more to the business traveler. However, prices are still reasonable, the staff are great, and the suites are a good choice for family stays, within easy reach of the Verizon Center.

Holiday Inn Central

MAP P2 ■ 1501 Rhode Island Ave at 15th St, NW ■ 1800-972-3159 ■ inn-dc.com ■ Dis. access ■ $
This downtown hotel has in-room Nintendo game consoles, which, added to the rooftop pool and cable TV and in-room movies, keep children entertained. Some oversized rooms are available. Dupont Circle and McPherson Square Metro stops are within walking distance.

The Liaison Capitol Hill

MAP R4 ■ 415 New Jersey Ave, NW ■ 202-638-1616 ■ affinia.com ■ Dis. access ■ $
Previously part of the Holiday Inn chain, this hotel has been well refurbished. The games, crafts, and outdoor pool provide plenty to keep children occupied. Under 12s dine free and under 19s stay free.

Courtyard Washington, DC/ Dupont Circle

MAP M1 ■ 1900 Connecticut Ave NW ■ 202-332-9300 ■ marriotthotels.com ■ Dis. access ■ $$
Conveniently located for the National Zoo, this hotel provides extra guestroom space and good services. The out-door pool is safe for kids, and there are free cookies in the lobby every afternoon.

Holiday Inn Capitol

MAP Q5 ■ 550 C St, SW ■ 202-479-4000 ■ hicapitoldc.com ■ Dis. access ■ $$
This hotel is a great choice for families – it offers an outdoor rooftop pool with a view; it's just one block away from the Air and Space Museum; and kids under 12 can eat for free. In addition, there is an on-site deli and guest laundry facilities.

Holiday Inn Georgetown

MAP 1 C1 ■ 2101 Wisconsin Ave NW, 20007 ■ 338-4600 ■ holidayinn. com ■ Dis. access ■ $$
Conveniently located just north of Georgetown, this seven-storey hotel features sleek decor and has an outdoor pool. John F's Market Café serves a buffet breakfast as well as dinner featuring Italian and American fare, and kids under 12 eat for free. It's also close to many specialty shops and restaurants, and operates a complimentary shuttle service to the Metro.

Omni Shoreham Hotel

MAP J5 ■ 2500 Calvert St, NW (at Connecticut Ave) ■ 202-234-0700 ■ omnihotels.com ■ Dis. access ■ $$
Close to Rock Creek Park and the National Zoo, this hotel's location makes it ideal for travelers with kids. Young guests are provided with activity backpacks on check-in.

The Quincy Hotel

MAP N3 ■ 1823 L St, NW ■ 202-223-4320 ■ thequincy.com ■ Dis. access ■ $$
In-room movies, treasure chests, sightseeing books, and pay-to-play Nintendo will appeal to the kids. Parents will appreciate the coffee-maker, fridge, microwave, and free Wi-Fi.

Washington Plaza

MAP P2 ■ 10 Thomas Circle, NW ■ 202-842-1300 ■ washingtonplaza hotel. com ■ Dis. access ■ $$
The beautifully landscaped grounds and resort-like hotel surround a large open-air pool. There is poolside dining in the summer, and a comfortable lounge featuring an open fire in winter.

J.W. Marriott

MAP P4 ■ 1331 Pennsylvania Ave, NW ■ 202-393-2000 ■ marriott. com/wasjw ■ Dis. access ■ $$$
Two blocks away from the White House, this hotel's great location minimizes walking distances for little feet. Child care is offered by prior arrangement.

Mid-Priced Hotels

Windsor Inn

MAP N1 ■ 1842 16th St, NW ■ 202-667-0300 ■ windsor-inn-dc.com ■ $–$$
Two 1920s buildings offer big hotel amenities in a charming, European-style environment. The main building is listed in the National Register of Historic Places, and has some marvelous Art Deco ornamentation. There is no elevator, but breakfast is complimentary.

Beacon Hotel and Corporate Quarters

MAP 3 B2 ■ 1615 Rhode Island Ave, NW (at 17th St), 20036 ■ 296-2100 ■ www.beaconhotelwdc. com ■ $$
The very comfortable rooms are decorated with cosmopolitan flair. Eight deluxe turret suites and 60 corporate suites come with fully equipped kitchens, high-speed Internet and web TV. The Beacon Bar & Grill restaurant serves food throughout the day, from breakfast to dinner.

Best Western Georgetown Hotel and Suites

MAP M3 ■ 1121 New Hampshire Ave, NW ■ 866-263-7212 ■ george towndchotel.com ■ Dis. access ■ $$
This is a simple downtown hotel, small and relatively quiet, given its popularity with families. The lobby has a working fireplace. All rooms are suites with kitchenette, and have free internet access. A free continental buffet breakfast is served daily.

Capitol Hill Hotel

MAP S5 ■ 200 C St, SE ■ 202-543-6000 ■ capitol hillhotel–dc.com ■ $$
This suites-only hotel was re-created from an apartment building, and the result is generously spacious rooms with kitchens. It's located near the Library of Congress, the US Capitol, and Eastern Market.

Embassy Suites Hotel at the Chevy Chase Pavilion

4300 Military Rd, NW (at Wisconsin & Western Aves), 20015 ■ 362-9300 ■ www.embassy suitesdcmetro.com ■ $$
Situated in the popular Chevy Chase shopping district, this all-suites hotel has easy access to a wide range of shops and restaurants, as well as the Friendship Heights Metro, all within the Chevy Chase Pavilion.

Breakfast is included in the tariff, and complimentary drinks and appetizers are served at a two-hour reception in Willie's Bar every evening.

L'Enfant Plaza Hotel

MAP Q5 ■ 480 L'Enfant Plaza SW ■ 202-484-1000 or 800-235-6397 ■ lenfantplazahotel.com ■ Dis. access ■ $$
The Mall is an easy two-block walk from here, and when visitors are not exploring Smithsonian museums, they can enjoy the amenities, such as the indoor pool, at this newly refurbished hotel (completed 2016), and its fine river views.

Georgetown Inn

MAP L2 ■ 1310 Wisconsin Ave, NW ■ 202-333-8900 ■ georgetowninn.com ■ $$
This hotel opened in 1961 at the height of John F. Kennedy's administration and the public's interest in Georgetown glamor, and it has been a fixture on the hotel scene ever since. All rooms are large and decorated in tasteful, elegant style, and offer free Wi-Fi. The Executive Rooms have a sitting area that is large enough to hold a meeting in.

Georgetown Suites

MAP L3 ■ 1000 30th St, NW ■ 202-759-4230 ■ georgetown suites.com ■ Dis. access ■ $$
Georgetown Suites offers a range of accommodation, from studios to a two-bedroom penthouse with a private patio that has Potomac River views. All have a separate sitting area and kitchen, as well as free Wi-Fi.

For a key to hotel price categories see p126

The Normandy Hotel
MAP M1 ▪ 2118 Wyoming Ave, NW ▪ 202-483-1350 ▪ doylecollection.com/washington ▪ $$

Located on a peaceful residential street, the Normandy has the feel of a bed and breakfast. Complimentary wine and cheese are served on Tuesday nights, and coffee, tea, and cookies are offered at other times.

Renaissance Washington, DC Downtown
MAP Q3 ▪ 999 9th St, NW ▪ 202-898-9000 ▪ marriot.com ▪ Dis. access ▪ $$

This large hotel, with over 800 rooms, is hard to miss thanks to its striking façade. It may be oriented toward business travelers, but is in a good tourist location in Penn Quarter.

Washington Marriott at Metro Center
MAP P3 ▪ 775 12th St, NW ▪ 202-737-2200 ▪ marriott.com ▪ Dis. access ▪ $$

An excellent downtown location. This smart, modern hotel with 459 rooms and suites still provides a personal touch. Fire and Sage restaurant serves seasonal food.

Budget Hotels

Adams Inn
MAP D3 ▪ 1746 Lanier Place, NW ▪ 202-745-3600 ▪ adamsinn.com ▪ $

A charming urban inn, with a very pretty garden. The hotel spreads over three 100-year-old townhouses. Some of the 27 rooms share a bath but have a sink in the room; all have free Wi-Fi.

Days Inn
4400 Connecticut Ave NW, Van Ness, 20008 ▪ 244-5600 ▪ www.dcdaysinn.com ▪ $

A convenient, affordable hotel, north of Cleveland Park near the Van Ness Metro, with clean rooms. Several restaurants are located nearby, including the Tesoro next door, which serves authentic Italian cuisine.

The District Hotel
MAP P2 ▪ 1440 Rhode Island Ave, NW ▪ 202-232-7800 ▪ districthotel.com ▪ $

This charming historic building, about six blocks from the White House, has been converted into 58 comfortable rooms with private bath that are popular with travelers on a limited budget.

Embassy Inn
MAP N2 ▪ 1627 16th St, NW ▪ 202-234-7800 ▪ embassy-inn-hotel-dc.com ▪ $

An elegant apartment house built in 1910 has been converted into a small hotel with 38 guest rooms, all with private bath. The hotel has been modernized, but many of the original features still remain, as do the tasteful façade and entranceway. Rooms are furnished with reproduction antiques and all come with free Wi-Fi, and a free Continental breakfast is offered daily.

Homewood Suites
MAP P2 ▪ 1475 Massachusetts Ave, NW ▪ 202-265-8000 ▪ homewood-suites.com ▪ $

This 175-room Hilton is ideal for extended stays as it is centrally located and offers good-sized accommodation, with separate living and sleeping areas and full kitchen. A free hot breakfast is served daily, and there is a 24/7 convenience store.

Hotel Harrington
MAP P4 ▪ 11th & E Sts, NW ▪ 202-628-8140 ▪ hotel-harrington.com ▪ $

At one time, this was the largest hotel in Washington, and it is still run by members of the founding family, a century later. It is popular with school groups, and also has outstanding family suites with two bathrooms.

The River Inn
MAP M3 ▪ 924 25th St, NW ▪ 202-337-7600 ▪ theriverinn.com ▪ Dis. access ▪ $–$$

This popular Foggy Bottom hotel has 126 suites, each with a full kitchen and a good-sized work or dining area. The name reflects the remarkable views of the river.

State Plaza Hotel
MAP M4 ▪ 2117 E St, NW ▪ 202-861-8200 ▪ stateplaza.com ▪ $

This all-suites hotel, located between the White House and the Kennedy Center, features a bistro with outdoor seating and a rooftop sun deck. Suites come with kitchens and have high-speed internet access.

The American Guest House
MAP F2 ▪ 2005 Columbia Rd, NW ▪ 202-588-1180 ▪ americanguesthouse.com ▪ $$

Spanning architecturally significant townhouses,

this guest house provides a comfortable base in an unbeatable neighborhood. The well-maintained rooms are handsomely furnished with plants, Oriental carpets, and period artwork. A free Continental breakfast is offered daily.

The Donovan
MAP P3 ▪ 1155 14th St, NW ▪ 202-737-1200 ▪ donovanhoteldc.com ▪ Dis. access ▪ $$
Located in the center of Downtown Washington, this hotel's fantastic rooftop bar and pool provide great views of the city. Rooms and public areas are stylishly chic, with a futuristic feel, and there's a hosted Wine Hour every evening.

Bed and Breakfast

Akwaaba Bed & Breakfast
MAP N2 ▪ 1708 16th St, NW ▪ 866-466-3855 ▪ akwaaba.com ▪ $
This charming B&B is located within walking distance of the White House. The historic townhouse has eight ensuite rooms, featuring premium linens, cable TV, and free Wi-Fi. Some rooms have a private balcony, Jacuzzi tub, and a decorative fireplace.

Taft Bridge Inn
MAP M1 ▪ 2007 Wyoming Ave, NW ▪ 202-387-2007 ▪ taftbridgeinn.com ▪ $
At this Inn, you'll find 12 beautifully decorated rooms in Victorian style. It's near the zoo and the vibrant Adams-Morgan neighborhood, and a free breakfast is included.

Chester A. Arthur Bed and Breakfast
MAP P2 ▪ 13th and P Sts, NW (at Logan Circle) ▪ 413-587-3009 ▪ chesterarthurhouse.com ▪ $$
This handsome and elegantly restored 19th-century townhouse offers over-sized rooms with antiques, cable TV, and internet access.

The Dupont at the Circle
MAP N2 ▪ 1604 19th St, NW ▪ 202-332-5251 ▪ dupontatthecircle.com ▪ $$
This charming Victorian townhouse offers six comfortable guest rooms and a one-bed apartment. The individually decorated bedrooms are furnished with antiques and luxury linens, and are renovated on a regular basis.

Embassy Circle Guest House
MAP F3 ▪ 2224 R St, NW ▪ 202-232-7744 ▪ dcinns.com/embassycircle ▪ $$
Rated one of the best bed and breakfasts in Washington, the Embassy Circle Guest House has 11 rooms, all with a private bath and shower. There are no TV sets or radios here, but there's plenty of entertainment within a five-minute walk in the Dupont Circle neighborhood. A complimentary buffet breakfast included.

The Inn at Dupont South
MAP N2 ▪ 1312 19th St, NW ▪ 202-359-8432 ▪ thedupontcollection.com ▪ $$
Just south of Dupont Circle, The Inn at Dupont South occupies a Victorian

rowhouse dating to 1855. Most of the rooms have a private bath and fireplace, and all have air-conditioning and wireless internet access. There's a private walled garden in which to enjoy afternoon tea.

Mt. Vernon Square Bed and Breakfast
MAP Q2 ▪ 400 M St, NW 20001 ▪ 888-399-5496 ▪ mvsbb.com ▪ $$
A restored townhouse with clean, spacious and comfortable rooms. Walking distance from several restaurants, bars, clubs, the Smithsonian Museum, National Mall and other sites. Ask for a quiet room as the traffic may bother some.

Swann House
MAP N1 ▪ 1808 New Hampshire Ave, NW ▪ 202-265-4414 ▪ swannhouse.com ▪ $$
Sometimes described as the best B&B in the city, this adorable 1883 mansion combines sparkling chandeliers and open fireplaces with all modern conveniences – Wi-Fi, private baths, and cable TV, and even a pool. Breakfast includes their home-made granola and gourmet hot dishes.

Mansion on O Street
MAP N2 ▪ 2020 O St, NW ▪ 202-496-2000 ▪ omansion.com ▪ $$$
This inn offers a variety of themed rooms, including a Graceland suite filled with memorabilia and the James Bond suite hidden behind a secret door. The layout is so striking that guests often regard the house as a sight in itself. Eclectic and charming.

For a key to hotel price categories see p126

General Index

Acknowledgments

Author

Ron Burke is the author or co-author of 19 books. A former Capitol Hill resident, he was born in the Washington, DC metropolitan area and has lived here most of his life.

Susan Burke lives in Virginia, where she worked on a daily newspaper for 20 years before becoming an editor for the Air Line Pilots Association. She is also a freelance editor for journals on labor, economics, and art conservation.

Additional contributor
Paul Franklin, Nancy Mikula

Publishing Director Georgina Dee

Publisher Vivien Antwi

Design Director Phil Ormerod

Editorial Michelle Crane, Rebecca Flynn, Rachel Fox, Fay Franklin, Fíodhna Ní Ghríofa, Freddie Marriage, Scarlett O'Hara, Marianne Petrou, Sally Schafer, Christine Stroyan

Revisions Emma Brady, Alice Powers, Ankita Sharma, Aakanksha Singh

Design Richard Czapnik, Marisa Renzullo, Jaynan Spengler

Picture Research Phoebe Lowndes, Susie Peachey, Ellen Root, Oran Tarjan

Cartography Subhashree Bharti, Simonetta Giori, Suresh Kumar, Casper Morris, John Plumer

DTP Jason Little, George Nimmo, Azeem Siddiqui, Joanna Stenlake

Production Nancy-Jane Maun

Factchecker Alice Powers

Proofreader Alyson Silverwood

Indexer Hilary Bird

Illustrator Chris Orr & Associates

First edition produced by Sargasso Media Ltd, London

Commissioned Photography: Paul Franklin, Rough Guides/Angus Osborn, Rough Guides/ Paul Whitfield, Kim Sayer, Giles Stokoe

Picture Credits

The publisher would like to thank the following for their kind permission to reproduce their photographs:
(**Key:** a-above; b-below/bottom; c-centre; f-far; l-left; r-right; t-top)

Alamy Images: David Coleman 57cb, 61tl, 65cl, 81tl; dbimages 101cl; Danita Delimont 49cl; Egglmages 73tr; Blaine Harrington III 4b; Marshall Ikonography 107br; National Geographic Image Collection 62ca; Nikreates 3tr, 106-7t, 116-7; North Wind Picture Archives 14tr, 42t; PAINTING/ Edgar Degas Dancers at the Barre. Circa 1900. Oil on canvas. Phillips Collection, Washington, D.C.

56tl; Chuck Pefley 106cl; Wiliam Perry 61bc; Stock Connection Blue 62b; Terry Smith Images 60t; Michael Ventura 4cla, 63cl; Visions of America/Purestock 111br; Harry Walker 63tr; Wiskerke 69b; YAY Media AS 43tr.

Brasserie Beck/RW Restaurant Group: Scott Suchman 97tr.

Clyde's Restaurant Group: 109br.

Corbis: 102tl; Bettmann 42br, 45bl, 102cr; Gary Carter 29tl; Design Pics/Robert Bartow 2tr, 40-1; Hulton-Deutsch Collection 43clb; Brooks Kraft 69tr; LOOP IMAGES/John Greim 4crb, 59br, 111t; National Geographic Creative/Scott S. Warren 56b; Oscar White 19tl; Richard T. Nowitz 58cb; PictureNet 4cr; Rudy Sulgan 51bl, 92-3; Underwood & Underwood 45cl; Terra/Fred Ward 28clb.

Dorling Kindersley: The Three Servicemen Statue © Frederick Hart /Vietnam Veterans Memorial Fund, 1984 86bl; US Navy Memorial "Lone Sailor" 1990 © Stanley Bleifeld, Washington DC 96c; John F. Kennedy Monument, 1971 ©Robert Berks Studios, Inc. All Rights reserved 98tl.

Dreamstime.com: Mira Agron 100cla; Americanspirit 36cla, 55cr; Annemario 72bl; Avmedved 16-17t, 87bl; Jon Bilous 31tr, 71clb, 113cl; Olga Bogatyrenko 12-3c; Brandon Bourdages © Vietnam Veterans Memorial Fund 50bl; Orhan Çam 79tr; Ken Cole 49tr; Cvandyke 4ca, 32cra, 64b, 96br; Dinhhang 11cla, 105br; Mesut Doğan 4clb; F11photo 4t, 28br, 52-3, 65br; Alexandre Fagundes De Fagundes 39bl, 51tr, 110tl; Julie Feinstein 60bl; Anton Foltin 74t; Frankljunior 70bl; Jose Gil 45tr; Richard Gunion 72tr; Patricia Agnes Hamilton 34-5c; Blaine Harrington III 3tl, 76-7; Izanbar 1, 2tl, 8-9, 74bl; Jemaerca 7crb; Wangkun Jia 7tr, 75tr; Kenk 75c; Kropic 35cr; Richie Lomba 46tr; Maisna66br; Mkopka 65tr, 112b; Mvogel 55tl; Nam Nguyen 71tr; Nickjene 100bl; William Perry 82br; Oleksii Popov/Franklin D. Roosevelt and his Dog Fala 1997 © Neil Estern 50t; Sophiejames 54bl; Steveheap 4cl; Vacclav 6cla.

Equinox Restaurant: 103bl.

Ford's Theatre: 93c, 94tl, Maxwell MacKenzie 48tr, 66t.

Fotolia: FD 15bc.

George Washington's Mount Vernon: 11bl, 36br, 36-7c.

Getty Images: Buyenlarge/Carol M. Highsmith 47clb; Hulton Archive 47tr; Hisham Ibrahim/ George Mason National Memorial 2002 Artist: Wendy M. Ross, Ross Sculpture Studio LLC, 6611 Landon Lane, Bethesda, Md. 20817 rosssculpture.com 58tl; Popperfoto 44cb; Tim Sloan 12bl; Chip Somodevilla 67tr; Daniel Stein 64tr; Julie Thurston Photography 80b; Universal Images Group 44tl; The Washington Post 67cl, 73cl, /Bill O'Leary 90br.

John Fluevog Shoes/Raw Information Group: 108tr.

Kramerbooks & Afterwords Cafe & Grill: Kate Headley 114tr.

Mary Evans Picture Library: Everett Collection 14br.

Monocle: Gary Hopkins 83tr.

NASA: Landsat 8 20tr.

Courtesy National Gallery of Art, Washington: George Washington portrait c.1850 by Rembrandt Peale, Gift of Mr. and Mrs. George W. Davison 14c; The Adoration of the Magi, c. , Fra Angelico c. 1395 - 1455, Lippi, Filippo, Fra c. 1406 - 1469. tempera on panel, 137.3 cm (54 1/16 in.) Samuel H. Kress Collection1952.2.2 / 24cla; Girl with the Red Hat c. 1665/1666, Johannes Vermeer 1632-1675, oil on panel, 22.8 x 18 cm (9 x 7 1/16 in.) support: 23.2 x 18.1 cm (9 1/8 x 7 1/8 in.) Andrew W. Mellon Collection 24crb; Wivenhoe Park, Essex, 1816. John Constable, oil on canvas, 56.1 x 101.2 cm (22 1/16 x 39 13/16 in.) Widener Collection1942.9.10 24bl; Right and Left, 1909, Winslow Homer, 1836-1910, oil on canvas, 71.8 x 122.9 cm (28 1/4 x 48 3/8 in.) Gift of the Avalon Foundation 25tl; George Washington c. 1803/1805, Gilbert Stuart 1755-1828. oil on canvas 73.6 x 61.4 cm (29 x 24 3/16 in.) Gift of Jean McGinley Draper 1954.9.2 25cra; The Dance Lesson c. 1879, Edgar Degas. oil on canvas. 38 x 88 cm (14 15/16 x 34 5/8 in.) Collection of Mr. and Mrs. Paul Mellon 26t; Sculpture garden featuring Graft, Roxy Paine 27b; 'Symphony in White, No. 1: The White Girl' 1862, James McNeill Whistler 1834 - 1903, oil on canvas, 213 x 107.9 cm, Harris Whittemore Collection 89tr.

Courtesy of the National Park Service: Abbie Row 19b.

National Museum of American History/© Smithsonian Institution: 10br, 22bl, 23clb.

National Museum of American History/ Smithsonian Institution: 22cra.

Restaurant Eve: 115crb.

Smithsonian's National Zoo: 33tl, 70t.

West End Bistro: 68clb.

White House Collection, Copyright White House Historical Association: Peter Vitale 16crb, 16bl, 17cr, 17br, 18tl, 18cr, 18bc

Jacket

Front and spine – **Dreamstime.com/Vacclav**
Back – **4Corners:** Massimo Borchi.

Pull out map cover

Dreamstime.com/Vacclav

All other images are: © Dorling Kindersley. For further information see www.dkimages.com.

Key to abbreviations in visitor information blocks:
Adm = admission charge; **Dis. Access** = disabled access.

Penguin
Random
House

Printed and bound in China

First published in Great Britain in 2003 by Dorling Kindersley Limited 80 Strand, London WC2R 0RL

Copyright 2003, 2016 © Dorling Kindersley Limited

A Penguin Random House Company

16 17 18 19 10 9 8 7 6 5 4 3 2 1

Reprinted with revisions 2004, 2005, 2006, 2007, 2008, 2009, 2010, 2011, 2012, 2013, 2014, 2016 (twice)

A CIP catalogue record is available from the British Library.

ISBN 978-0-2412-0919-6

MIX
Paper from responsible sources
FSC™ C018179

SPECIAL EDITIONS OF DK TRAVEL GUIDES

DK Travel Guides can be purchased in bulk quantities at discounted prices for use in promotions or as premiums. We are also able to offer special editions and personalized jackets, corporate imprints, and excerpts from all of our books, tailored specifically to meet your own needs.

To find out more, please contact:

in the US
specialsales@dk.com

in the UK
travelguides@uk.dk.com

in Canada
specialmarkets@dk.com

in Australia
penguincorporatesales@ penguinrandomhouse.com.au

Selected Street Index